You Don't Look Like An Ultra Runner

From Obsessive Twitcher to Unlikely Ultrarunner, Negotiating Life with a Bipolar Brain

By Tristan Reid

Contents

Act One - Details 1

Act Two – Bipolar Birding 9

Act Three – Birding Globe 35

Act Four - Unworked 85

Act Five - Tattoomania 109

Act Six – You don't look like an ultrarunner 122

Act Seven - Mania 158

Act Eight – Anxiety Tsunami 187

Act Nine – Music Therapy 208

Act Ten - Challenge 212

Appendix A – Mental Health Resources 230

Appendix B – Birding Resources 232

Appendix C – My Bird List 235

Appendix D – Running Resources 247

Big Thanks 248

The Author 250

Act One
Detail

It is fair to say that I have packed quite a lot into my life so far, it has been a real adventure! I have a lot of great and challenging experiences to share with you, but first I need to give some context that may well explain some of those more unusual choices I have made as I tried to negotiate the complexities of my life.

Before I continue with my story, it is important to give you a trigger warning. Although this book does contain a lot of exciting adventuring, I will also be touching on mental illness topics such as depression, mania, death, and suicidal ideation. My description of all these very serious subjects, could possibly act as a trigger to some people already struggling with mental illness symptoms. For anyone who may be affected by this, I have put some useful numbers and resources in the appendices of this book.

Talking about mental illness was historically not the 'done thing,' particularly if you happened to be male. This attitude must be a contributing factor as to why male suicide rates are still sadly so disproportionately high in the UK. Things are changing for the better, but this is a slow process and people are still dying unnecessarily. This is why we must feel free and able to speak openly about mental illness, and how we manage or struggle with our mental health.

I knew that there was something a little different about me from quite an early age. I did not really know what it was that made me feel so different, but I could see clearly that other people that I engaged with, really didn't see things the same way as I seemed to. They did not think like me, and they really didn't understand me. It was not just strangers; friends and school colleagues I found it difficult to relate to. Frustratingly, I struggled connecting with my siblings too.

I spent a lot of my time on my own by choice, because this was the easiest and most comfortable choice for me. It was not a happy choice, as it left me feeling isolated and at times, painfully lonely. Some of these perceived differences to my personality compared to others, could have been explained by my less than conventional upbringing but, as I would learn later in life, there was a far more significant reason for all of this.

Even as a child, I would have frequent periods of darkness. Episodes I now recognise as depression. I never spoke about my depression back then, partly because I was not sure if it was something everyone one felt, and because talking about feelings was simply not encouraged. In fact, it was not until 2008 that I got an official diagnosis of clinical depression along with general and social anxiety disorder. My initial treatment was a selective serotonin reuptake inhibitor (SSRI) antidepressant medication called Citalopram. This was latterly followed up with some cognitive behavioural therapy. As time went on, it was becoming clear that my condition was deteriorating, despite being completely compliant with my prescribed medication and therapy.

During the first half of 2016, some eight years after my initial diagnosis, I was re-diagnosed with bipolar affective disorder. I did not have any real understanding of what bipolar was. The only references I had been often inaccurate and extreme stigmatising representations on film and television, such as Glen Close's character in Fatal Attraction.

After speaking at length with my psychiatrist and reading up on the condition, things started to make a lot more sense to me. The most simplistic way I can describe Bipolar to someone, is to ask them to visualise their mood as a sliding scale numbered from one to ten, with one representing the extreme low end and ten representing the extreme high end. People that do not live with bipolar will usually have a mood that ranges between four and seven on this scale, whilst someone who does live with bipolar will have a mood range that can travel the full length of the scale. Bipolar is a lot more complex than that though, and one person's symptoms will not necessarily be the same as somebody else's symptoms. Not only that, but as outlined by NICE (the National Institute for Health and Care Excellence), there are three distinctive types of bipolar.

Bipolar 1 is categorised by someone who has experienced at least one manic episode that has lasted a week or more, some depressive episodes (though not in all cases) and sometimes some psychosis.

Bipolar 2 is characterised by someone who has experienced an episode of hypomania that has lasted for four days or more and at least one depressive episode.

Cyclothymia is characterised by someone who has experienced both hypomanic and depressive episodes over a period of two years or more. The symptoms are not usually as extreme as in Bipolar 1 and 2, but this is still a serious condition.

This book should not be considered a self-help book of any kind, I'm not qualified for that! Whilst I would never claim to be an expert on bipolar, I think I can consider myself to be well versed on my own symptoms. Throughout the years, since my diagnosis, things have been far from easy. It is my hope that anyone with bipolar will draw some comfort or understanding from this honest and personal account.

After my diagnosis I was prescribed my first bipolar specific medication, an antipsychotic called quetiapine. Well, you know you are winning at life when you're needing to take antipsychotics! This was a serious medication, considering I had to get an electrocardiogram (ECG) before I could start it. I had to titrate up to a therapeutic dose gradually, but I was soon taking the prescribed amount. My first experiences of this medicine were not particularly positive. This drug made me very sleepy throughout the day. This was not the quality of life I could cope with for a prolonged length of time.

The psychiatrist then prescribed me a slow-release version, which solved that issue. I was taking quetiapine for quite a while, but not only was it not helping me mentally, but I was also gaining a significant amount of weight. My psychiatrist suggested we tried something different. This was the beginning of many years of trial and error with multiple tablet combinations. You see, it's not a case of one size fits all with bipolar medication. What works for one does not necessarily work for all. Not only that, but people's tolerances of side effects can vary greatly. I tried many different combinations of antipsychotics, antidepressants and mood stabilisers over the following months and years. These included Fluoxetine, Lamotrigine, Valproic Acid, Aripiprazole and Venlafaxine. One of the most counterproductive medications I tried was the antipsychotic, Olanzapine. I took this for around five months. It did not help reduce my bipolar symptoms, but it was instrumental in me gaining over 5 stone (32 kg) in weight. Some antipsychotics like olanzapine can increase the chances of weight gain because of several factors. Raised blood glucose levels and metabolism dysfunction are caused by severe disruption to some essential gut bacteria. Additionally, the medication can alter the way the body stores fat and it can cause fluctuations in some hormone levels as an increase in prolactin and reduction in testosterone. This combination is a recipe for weight gain. The most noticeable side effect I experienced was a significantly increased appetite and cravings for fatty and sugary foods. It did not seem to matter how much I ate; I was always hungry. I am still trying to shift the weight I gained from my time on this medication six years later.

Having been told I had this psychiatric illness; I did what I usually do in new situations and disappeared into the internet maze to find out as much as I could about what bipolar is and how it would affect my life both in the short-term and in the long-term. Knowledge is power and all that. Sometimes though, ignorance is bliss! The main reason I needed to know all that I could about the disorder was to help me manage my life better and perhaps find some sort of belonging. I joined quite a few bipolar forums and Facebook groups to help me better understand what I was having to deal with. However, rather than finding a community I could relate to, I just felt even more isolated. I am generalising a bit here, but I found two types of members there; people who had quite extreme symptoms that needed help or those who were evangelical about going medication free.

These engagements were not helpful to me at that stage of my life. In fact, they were counterproductive. I could not find anyone I could relate to, which welcomed back my old 'friend,' imposter syndrome! Despite feeling this way, I was not completely on my own, thankfully. I had trustworthy, caring people like Kathleen and Sam who I could confide in as well as certain family members. This was, and continues to be, essential for my wellbeing. Of course, they do not fully understand what happens in my brain (who does), but their non-judgmental and caring qualities are always hugely comforting.

I continued researching bipolar and conditions with similar features and, after chatting about things to another friend, I had convinced myself that my bipolar diagnosis was wrong. I believed that I may in fact have complex post-traumatic stress disorder (CPTSD). At this point in my care, I had seen three different psychiatrists, all of whom had asked a lot of serious and personal questions and all three had given me the same diagnosis of bipolar affective disorder. One of them gave the more specific diagnosis of bipolar Despite being aware of this, I was still far from convinced, so I decided to share my concerns with my psychiatrist. He did take me seriously (or humoured me at least) and after a lengthy conversation, which included a lot more heavy questions, he told me that he was adamant that I did not have CPTSD and that my original diagnosis of bipolar was still correct. I accepted this, for a period at least.

The bipolar symptoms I suffer from are long depressive periods interspersed with shorter episodes of hypomania or mania. I rarely have any periods of 'normal' balanced states. To be honest, I might not even recognise it if it happened anyway. As I have stumbled through life I have got used to these lengthy periods of depression. In fact, compared to mania, it is oddly comforting. This is through familiarity and, contrasting with mania, I feel like I have control. Subconsciously I know that it may well facilitate my exit from a far too difficult life.

The level of depression can swing between moderate to severe, rarely mild. Severe depression is the most dangerous form to me as it comes with symptoms that include suicidal ideation. This is a difficult one to deal with as it does make logical sense to me at the time. It manifests as intrusive thoughts that I have no control over. Often these thoughts are shouted at me by my own voice, my inner dialogue if you like. I rarely act on these thoughts, having only seriously planned or tried to end my life on a handful of occasions. I have some robust safeguards in place that usually stops me from succeeding in these endeavours. Namely my children.

Children whose parent dies from suicide are three times more likely to die the same way. This is obviously something that I would not want to happen. Whilst this does stop me from making the finite decision, it also makes these episodes a whole lot more difficult to cope with. In addition to those horrible dark thoughts, my depression also feels like I am shrouded in a dark cloud that follows me everywhere and keeps me feeling uncomfortably numb with very low motivation, very low personal self-worth, poor or non-existent self-care and massively reduced energy. My speech can become noticeably slow and although I might not always be potentially suicidal, I am frequently hoping for a terminal physical illness or engaging in risky behaviours that would put my life in danger.

The terminology of episodes from the higher end of the spectrum are mania or hypomania. Whilst I understand that hypomania is the less extreme version of mania, I have always been uncertain at what point exactly hypomania becomes mania. I tend to refer to my episodes on the higher mood range using the more general name of mania. Although my manic episodes can be varied in their appearance, they do have some identifiable components in common.

The early signs tend to be an increase in energy, apparent reduced need for sleep, getting hyper fixated about a particular subject that I have generally never shown much interest in before and sometimes (but not always) talking at an increased cadence. Grandiose thoughts do frequently feature, and this can involve putting myself (and sometimes others) in danger due to risky behaviour or committing myself to challenges that I have no business taking on. Out of control spending is certainly the behaviour that can have the biggest impact on my family. It is not unusual for me to max out credit cards or empty my bank account without a thought of consequence during a spending spree.

The thing you should understand about me when I am exhibiting these extreme moods is that I am always oblivious to the fact that I am doing anything unusual. This condition inhibits rational thinking at times. Language is key, particularly when describing bipolar. Some people consider themselves lucky to have the

7

condition. They may consider that it gives them a 'superpower' that makes them stand out from the crowd. I can certainly understand that way of thinking. I try to be careful not to refer to bipolar as a disease or illness because of those ideas. However, I personally believe that any condition that constantly tries to kill you, must be a disease.

People with bipolar frequently ask themselves this question; if there was a cure for bipolar, would you take it? Surprisingly, most people say they would not accept the cure. I can understand why that is such a common response. The elevated moods that come with the condition can feel amazing and also direct you into some incredible experiences. For me the condition causes too much pain to me and those close to me, I would have to take the cure despite the positives.

That is the heavier subject matter done for the time being you will be glad to hear, I'm sure! Now for some bipolar-fuelled adventures...

Act Two
Bipolar Birding

My interest in wildlife began when I was a young child; I had a fascinated inquisitive mind when it came to the natural world. I don't know exactly where this originated from, but it was encouraged to some extent by my parents. One thing that featured consistently throughout my life was becoming hyper focused various subjects. Birding, perhaps the most accessible group of fauna, rapidly became my big obsession for many years. Birds really gave me the escapism that I needed. Living in southwest Cornwall I really did not know what new species I would see, from one day to the next. Watching birds had got me hooked and over the years I had happily immersed myself in the culture of twitching. Twitchers are birders who travel all over their country to try and see rare birds. Although rarities would eventually become my driving force, I always got immense pleasure from seeing common, and scarce birds that bred in Britain.

My favourite UK breeding bird is the European Nightjar. Nightjars are fascinating species that breed across most of Europe (excluding the far north) and the Palearctic region, as far east as Mongolia and northwest China. They are migratory across their whole range, wintering in sub-Saharan Africa.

The European Nightjar was formally quite widespread in Britain but due to fragmentation of habitat caused by agriculture and deforestation, the species has a very restricted and scattered distribution. Recent surveys have indicated that there are over 4,500 territorial males currently present in the British countryside.

The Nightjar is a very cryptic and mystical bird. One of its historical names is the Common Goatsucker. This refers to an old and erroneous theory that they suckled from goats at night, causing the mammals to go dry!

My first observations of European Nightjar was on a lowland heathland in Norfolk. As the species is active during crepuscular and nocturnal hours, their mystical reputation is understandable. Seeing nightjars on their breeding grounds is quite an immersive and multi-sensory experience. I remember standing on the heath as the light was fading after a baking hot day. The earthy smell of the ground was distinctively pleasant. There was a lull in activity as the diurnal birds ceased to sing. The only birds noticeable were the tweeting and grunting of Woodcock patrolling their territories and the reeling of a Grasshopper Warbler from somewhere deep in the scrub. Suddenly, in the last of the daylight I heard this distinctive and evocative, sustained, low churring trill emanating from the top of a birch tree. There on the tree was the weirdest looking bird I had ever seen. The nightjar had streaky grey, brown, and buff plumage, superficially like the equally strange Wryneck.

I had a good view of the bird's face, so could make out the contrasting pale moustachial stripe. After a while, the Nightjar took flight along with a few others that had previously been hidden. Seeing them in flight is just incredible. With their long wings and long tail, they look almost falcon like as they carve through the air hunting for moths and other insects. Although unlike falcons, they scoop up their prey in their wide gaping mouths.

The nightjars were not just feeding when I saw them, it was amazing to see them swooping overhead, flashing their white wing patches, and occasionally clapping their wings as part of their display flight.

I have been lucky to see and hear Eurasian Nightjars at several locations in Britain and it has always been an incredible experience. Not all my encounters with this species have been in fading light. It is unusual to see nightjars away from the breeding grounds in Britain, but sometimes being in the right place at the right time really does pay dividends. One autumn at Spurn Point in East Yorkshire I managed to be at the reserve when a Nightjar had been located on the headland. It was a special moment watching a migrating Eurasian Nightjar flying around the peninsula in daylight.

Before the obsession of twitching really took hold of my life, I was more than content spending time birding on various local patches, where my main hope was to find my own rare birds. I put in a lot of time and effort doing this, and on occasion I did find something interesting. I was not a serial rarity finder, but when I did see something unusual on my patch, it was always exciting!

Some of my favourite finds are Coues's Arctic Redpoll (Foula, 1996), American Golden Plover (Cumbria, Anthorn, 2005), Melodious Warbler (East Yorkshire, Spurn, 2000), 3 Pallas's Warblers (Scottish Borders, St Abb's Head, 1996), Great Reed Warbler (Scottish Borders, St Abb's Head, 1997),

Although I went on my first twitch in 1986, when I was only eleven years old, I did not really graduate into a fully-fledged twitcher until 1999. A vital part of twitching is keeping a list to keep track of the number of species seen. Back then, seeing 400 species in Britain or Britain and Ireland, was considered the big challenge. Nowadays many keen twitchers have surpassed 500 species and the keenest are approaching 600! For me at the time, my target was to see 400 species in Britain and Ireland, and I had no expectation beyond that.

By the time I stopped birding and twitching, in the late 2010's, I had seen 438 species in Britain and Ireland. This was not a groundbreaking number, but some incredibly beautiful and rare birds, as well as many fantastic experiences helped to build that list. I have placed my entire British and Irish list at the back of this book, should you wish to look at it in more detail. There are many amazing memories attached to huge number of birds on my list.

I have been lucky to see quite a range of birds during my time twitching. Some of my favourites are, Myrtle Warbler (Co. Durham, High Shincliffe, 2014), Sociable Lapwing (Suffolk, Minsmere, 2014. Dresser's Eider (Co. Donegal, Glassagh Bay, 2011), Two-barred Warbler (North Yorkshire, Filey, 2006), Snowy Egret (Ayrshire, Stevenson, 2002), White-throated Robin (Cleveland, Hartlepool Headland, 2011) and Black Lark (Anglesey, South Stack, 2003).

The final two rarities are my absolute favourites, and these both require a little more context. The first of these is the Eastern Crowned Warbler that was located at Trow Quarry in Co. Durham during autumn 2009. This is where one of my poorest decisions came into play. This was the first record of this species ever in Britain. I had to see it. So that day I did. The problem with this was that very same day that was the due date for our third child. I had convinced myself that it would be fine, it was unlikely to be 'the day' and I was only two hours away at worse. Besides, I had been present for the other two's birth, so it wouldn't have been the end of the world, would it? Looking back now, with a leveller head, it breaks my heart to think of how Kathleen must have felt!

As you would expect for a first for Britain, the Trow Quarry location was busy with twitchers. It was quite funny when the local news journalists turned up, we could see several birders diving into bushes. Presumably to avoid being seen on TV because they'd likely skipped work to see the bird! Thankfully, we did not have to wait long before we were watching the absolutely stunning Eastern

Crowned Warbler. The bird was quite large for a *phylloscopus* warbler and showed slender pale double wing-bars and bright flared supercilium, superficially reminiscent of an Arctic Warbler. However, the greener toned upperparts and dark olive crown dissected by a pale central crown stripe made the bird very straightforward to identify.

This Eastern Crowned Warbler was an extraordinarily long way away from its natural range. The species breeds in temperate and taiga forests across eastern regions of Siberia from the Argun River east and southwards into western Northeast China, central Szechwan, the Korean peninsula, and Japan. They migrate to eastern areas of India and Bangladesh eastwards to Java.

I am pleased to say that luck was on my side that day as things worked out okay in the end. Our third daughter, Thea, was born the next day and I was there of course. A new family member and an Eastern Crowned Warbler in the space of two days. Not my finest moment and very much a close one, but what a double!

The second of these two standout rare birds that I have been very lucky to see, was the Blue-winged Warbler on Cape Clear Island in Co. Cork (Ireland), during September 2000.

Whilst I was studying at Bishop Burton College, I was attending a very dry statistics lecture, when my pager received a 'mega alert.' I am paraphrasing here, but the message read something like 'Blue-winged Warbler in Cotters Garden on Cape Clear Island.' I looked across to Ian, to see if he'd received the message, he glanced back at me, with a confused expression, so I knew he had!

During the break, I stood outside the lecture theatre, looked at Ian, and we both said, 'what the hell is a Blue-winged Warbler,' or words to that effect! I can only speak for myself here in and I certainly would not have called myself an expert in anything, but I had built up enough experience and knowledge at this point to be aware of what species of birds had been recorded in Britain and Ireland, and what species were eagerly anticipated. I was sure that the Blue-winged Warbler was not any of these. I was aware of the Golden-winged Warbler, a species of North American wood warbler, recorded once in Britain. My assumption was that the Blue-winged Warbler was a close relative of that species. After a bit of research, we confirmed that the Blue-winged Warbler was indeed a closely related species to the more familiar and still very rare Golden-winged Warbler. This was extremely exciting news indeed.

The Blue-winged Warbler breeds in southern Ontario and the eastern United States, wintering in southern Central America. The bird was not only a first record for Ireland, but the first record for the Western Palearctic. The Western Palearctic is a biogeographical realm that includes Europe, north Africa, northern and central areas of the Arabian Peninsula and into some of temperate Asia as far east as the Urals.

Well, you know the score by now! I was soon on my way to Ireland with Ian and a few of his friends, which included Paul Hackett, someone I would get to know well over the coming years. We drove into Wales to take the car ferry across to Ireland. Then it was a fair old drive to Baltimore in County Cork. We slept in the car until morning, where we were welcomed onto a charter boat by some local Irish birders. The boat took us across to Cape Clear in immersive weather conditions!

Cape Clear is an absolutely iconic island within the birding community. Once we had landed on the island, the grim weather thankfully did clear up a little, so we did not have to wait long before we were enjoying incredible views of the Western Palaearctic's first Blue-winged Warbler. This was an amazing bird to see! It was a very striking warbler, with its bright yellow underparts, yellowy-olive head and back, which contrasted beautifully with its substantial pointy dark bill, black eye-stripe, and blue-grey wings. Could things get any better? Well yes, they could, and they did!

We managed to see our first Red-eyed Vireo in Cotter's Garden, in the same 'scope view as the Blue-winged Warbler. What a place! The local birders and bird observatory staff were very welcoming and hospitable. This really added to the incredible experience of my second visit to Ireland. Once back on the mainland, we visited Galley Head, where we had good views of a Yellow-browed Warbler. After a night in Kerry, we made our way back home. The Blue-winged Warbler was undoubtedly the rarest bird that I'd ever seen, and this trip was one I would never forget. The exquisite Blue-winged Warbler sits, quite deservedly, at the top of my favourite rare birds that I've seen in Britain or Ireland.

Aside from out and out twitches, I took many birding weekends away or birding holidays within Britain and Ireland. Rather than giving you a blow-by-blow account of every trip I've ever been on, here is a taste of my top five exciting adventures.

Derek Charles is a great friend of mine, besides being a decent human being, he is a great birder, bird finder and gull guru based across the Irish Sea. I had communicated with him for quite a few years over gull identification and the like. He is one of those kind and generous people that you rarely meet in life. I had the pleasure of visiting Derek in Ireland for some memorable birding trips.

Chris joined me for most of the trips. There are some very iconic locations in Ireland that have hosted some interesting species. These are sites like Killybegs and Nimmo's Pier and it was fantastic to make the pilgrimage to these fascinating areas. During our numerous trips we managed to see some really exciting birds such as Thayer's Gull, Kumlien's Gulls, Iceland Gulls, Glaucous Gulls, Ring-billed Gulls, American Herring Gull, Forster's Tern, King Eiders, Stejeneger's Scoter, Surf Scoter, Barrow's Goldeneye, Lesser Scaup, Richardson's Goose, and an unexpected Central

Asian Lesser Whitethroat. Not a bad haul and there are so many incredible memories attached to every one of those birds!

One of the most magical trips away I did with some of the Spurn regulars, was down to my adopted home-county of Cornwall. I was joining rare bird magnet Adam Hut, Gareth Picton, and their friend Paul Freestone for a couple of days in Kernow focusing round the iconic Scillonian pelagic (the term pelagic refers to anything relating to open ocean). In birding terms, a pelagic is simply a boat trip that specifically searches for seabirds using a scent lure known as chum. The chum is a pretty gruesome mixture of squashed sardines, other fish and fish oils. The smell, though tempting to pelagic birds, would put you off your breakfast!

After leaving Spurn, we began the 440 or so miles to south-western Cornwall. Gareth thought it would be hilarious to ask me a random question every time (EVERY TIME) he saw me dozing off! So, as I'm sure you can imagine, I arrived in Cornwall feeling not quite as well rested as I had hoped.

Our first stop was to my old patch of Marazion Marsh. I don't remember seeing anything significant on the bird front, but the bright sunshine meant there was some *odonata* to see. Alongside the commoner species, we got magnificent views of Broad-bodied Chasers, Golden-ringed Dragonfly and the superbly named Beautiful Demoiselle.

The Scillonian is the passenger ferry that takes people and supplies to and from Penzance and the Isles of Scilly. It is a flat-bottomed boat, which enables it to manoeuvre into the relatively shallow waters of the harbour at Hugh town on St Mary's. The downside to this, is that the ferry rolls about on the waves, particularly in rough seas. It notoriously makes passengers seasick, which has earned it the nickname of the 'sickonian'! I was understandably nervous and apprehensive about spending around fourteen hours on this boat on the open ocean.

The only previous experience I had of the Scillonian was when I went on a school trip to the islands. We travelled on rough seas, and I've never felt so ill in my life. What made it worse was having to wait for hours offshore for the storm to pass before we could disembark on St Mary's. As it happened, I really had nothing to worry about because for the duration of the pelagic it was flat-calm seas and bright sunshine.

Whilst these were not the best conditions for bringing in large numbers of seabirds, it was definitely a more enjoyable voyage. The birding was actually surprisingly good. We saw Grey Phalarope, Sabine's Gull, Sooty Shearwaters, Manx Shearwaters and European Storm Petrels.

The main reason people elect to sign up for this pelagic is to see the locally rare, globally widespread Wilson's Petrel. This species is a real speciality of the southwest approaches. We were not to be disappointed as we got excellent views of at least three individuals.

The star bird for me, however, was a Great Shearwater. This striking large shearwater was a long way from its south Atlantic home and just spectacular to see. Interestingly for me, the overall highlights of the pelagic were not birds at all. They came in the form of a fish and a reptile! The fish was the superbly weird Atlantic Ocean Sunfish. At around 1.8 meters (5ft 11in) in length and 2.5 meters (8ft 2in) from fin to fin, they are huge fish that can weigh up to 1000kg (157st 7lb). In fact, they are the second largest bony fish found on planet earth! Atlantic Ocean Sunfish feed on a variety of small fish, squid, jellyfish, salps, and crustaceans.

They dive into deep waters to find their prey, which is why we were seeing them on the surface of the sea, lying sideways, looking like a huge grey disc with a massive fin flapping through the water. The consensus is that they loaf on the sea surface to bask in the sun after spending time in the colder deep waters. It was both incredible and fascinating to get such amazing views of these alien looking super fish.

We were very lucky to see three or four sunfish during the duration of the pelagic. Although we saw such spectacular mammals as Pilot Whales, Fin Whale, and Risso's Dolphin, the most incredible sighting of the pelagic for me personally was the six Leatherback Turtles that we managed to see. I had no expectations of seeing any turtles on this trip, they weren't even on my radar! The reality of seeing one, let alone six, was, well it was emotional. To me the Leatherback Turtle symbolises survival against all odds and freedom.

I've heard about people bursting into tears when seeing wild elephants for the first time, although I didn't cry outwardly when I saw my first turtle, I definitely felt the emotion. The Leatherback Turtle at up to 1.8 meters (5ft 11in) in length and 500kg (78st 10Ib) in weight are absolutely colossal. In fact, not only are they the largest extant turtle on the planet, but they are the heaviest reptiles outside of the crocodilians. All the Leatherback Turtles that I saw were large adults, so definitely at the upper end of the species size and weight. I had no idea that they even got that huge. I don't think I can adequately convey in words how much of an incredible experience it was seeing these sea reptiles, but it still rates as one of my best lifetime experiences so far. What a momentously incredible trip!

Ian and I spent the best part of two weeks camping on the small islands of Out Skerries. I had visited this place only once before, to see a Great Snipe, so I was anticipating great things. Out Skerries is an exceptional area. The scenery is fantastic, and the locals are welcoming and friendly. What is not to like? From a birding perspective it is a real gem. The island is often first landfall for birds blown in from the east on Shetland and its diminutive size means that it is easily to cover in a day. Staying in a tent was an interesting challenge during south easterly gales and persistent rain, but the birding was great. Some of the highlights from this trip included Black-headed Bunting, Red-throated Pipit, Rustic Bunting, Olive-backed Pipit, Bluethroats, Red-breasted Flycatcher and Yellow-breasted Bunting. The experience of seeing huge flocks of Snow Buntings and winter thrushes was also very spectacular.

The most frustrating and intriguing sighting we observed was of a species of flycatcher on the church wall. At the time we knew it was not a Red-breasted, Spotted or Pied Flycatcher, but we didn't have a real clue of what it was. This was the days before I played at wildlife photography, so we had no evidence to work from when we got home. That said we were convinced that what we had seen was most likely an Asian Brown Flycatcher, an absolute mega rarity. Unfortunately, we had no way of proving this, so it had to be filed away as the one that got away!

This was an interesting introduction to birding politics perhaps. I submitted identification description reports to the British Birds Rarities Committee (BBRC) for the Red-throated Pipit, Olive-backed Pipit and Yellow-breasted Bunting. I also submitted a description of the suspected Asian Brown Flycatcher, but as a flycatcher not confidently identified to species. This seemed the most honest approach. Unfortunately, all my submitted records were rejected as not proven. Although this was disappointing to me, it certainly was expected. During my stay on Out Skerries some of the birders I was spending time with had made a rather big identification error with a bird that they had found. Although I had nothing to do with the situation, I suspect that my bird identification prowess had been tarnished by association. I wasn't overly concerned about this result as I certainly wasn't going to let the opinions of people, I didn't really know put a downer on what had been an amazing experience.

The only thing that irked me a little was that no-one from the BBRC gave me any feedback on the flycatcher. If nothing else, I would have welcomed the opportunity to learn something regarding the identification process. This whole experience had helped put my birding into context. I was happy with my identification ability. There was, and is, always room for improvement and the key was to be always honest. I birded for my own pleasure, no-one else's. If a committee somewhere threw out my records, it really did not matter. If I was confident with my own identification, then that was good enough for me. I was a lot more selective with my BBRC rare bird submissions after that.

Out Skerries was an amazing place to spend time on. Staying in a tent for two weeks in high winds and rain was interesting. Probably the funniest thing about that was the continual boasts from Ian, stating that his tent had been tested on Everest. The thing was the only tent that lasted the two weeks was my cheap budget tent from Millets!

All that grim weather however, brought an amazing selection of birds which allowed me to find a scarce bird in the most chilled way in the history of birding! I was leaning on a bridge chatting to Ian, when I glanced over my left shoulder only to notice a Red-breasted Flycatcher perched on a rock in the stream. I casually told Ian, who quickly got on to the bird before it flew off downstream. I was like 'The Fonze,' only younger! I think if you are on any of the Shetland Islands in autumn with perfect conditions you will believe you are on the frontier of rare bird possibilities. Really, anything could show itself to you.

When news of a white-phase Gyrfalcon in Cornwall broke, we got a minibus full of like-minded birders together and took full advantage of our newly discovered bird club perks at Bishop

Burton College! This trip would turn out to be one of my most amazing twitches ever. We got a plan together and began our overnight journey to the south-west.

To add to the adventure, I was really happy that Kath was accompanying me too. It's around four hundred and ten miles from Bishop Burton College to Gwennap Head but, thanks to Mark's driving skills, we made good time, and we arrived in Cornwall the following morning.

The Gyrfalcon is a big falcon. In fact, it owns the title of the largest falcon species in the world. From tail tip to head it measures in between 48 to 65cm (19 to 25in) with a wingspan ranging from 110 to 160cm (3.6 to 5.2ft). The females are larger than the males, hence the broad range in biometrics. The Gyrfalcon breeds near the Arctic coasts and tundra habitat across the islands of northern North America as well as throughout the Euro-/Siberian region. The bird we were anticipating seeing was a white-phase Gyrfalcon, so it almost certainly originated from Greenland.

We disembarked the minibus and most of us hastily hiked up the coastal path close to the bird's favoured cliffs. On our way along the path, we sighted the magnificent falcon as it flew towards and then over the carpark. I had not anticipated how large this bird was until this point. This was illustrated perfectly by the handful of birders left in the carpark. We'd alerted them to the fact that the bird was flying over their heads. We instantly heard the delectable Chingford accent of young Rich Cope, shouting 'where is it from the Herring Gull?' The instantaneous choral response was simply 'it is the Herring Gull'! a beautiful moment made all the sweeter by the fact that our whole contingent had successfully connected with the Gyr.

The falcon appeared to fly back towards the cliffs, so we continued along the path towards the cliffs. We were then treated to prolonged and close views of the Gyrfalcon as it sat on the cliffs unconcerned about our palpable excitement. What an amazing bird to have the opportunity to see. Even Kath was impressed with this experience! Whilst all of us would have happily spend hours more enjoying the Gyr, we were in Cornwall and there was a lot of high-quality birds to try and see. So, we packed ourselves back into the bus and made our way to some familiar areas to me; Marazion, overlooking St Michael's Mount, and Mounts Bay.

Here we got some great views of a female King Eider. This was only the second record of this species in Cornwall and my second record of the species in Cornwall. Given that most identified King Eiders that turn up in Britain are drakes, it must be very unusual that both Cornish records, which were fourteen years apart, were females. I was of course pleased to see this King Eider on my old patch, but I definitely hoped I would see a less subtle drake one day! Next, we made our way on to Hayle and the Hayle Estuary in particular. It was great to be back there, it really was where I cut my birding teeth. The estuary was busy with birds, and it was fantastic to search through the commoner species to try and of the scarcer birds.

We did not do too badly as we got views of Spoonbill, Ring-billed Gull, Green-winged Teal and only my second American Wigeon. This was a delightful selection of scarcities that added a bit more depth to our already incredible day in my adopted home county. We celebrated our successful first day of the trip with a few drinks (well, a lot, for me anyway) in a weird nightclub that just looked like a shop, in St Ives. After a good night's sleep, we were on the road again, for the second part of our trip that was mostly in Devon.

After the expected slog of a journey from south-west Cornwall to Devon, we arrived at Stover Country Park, which is situated close to Newton Abbot. It did not take long before we were enjoying marvellous views of our second major rarity of the trip, a Sora Rail. This striking crake with its grey, brown, and white specked barred underparts, bright yellow stubby beak, and black mask breeds from southern Alaska, throughout the United States and into the northern Baja region of Mexico. They migrate to the West Indies and northern South America for the winter. It is incredible that a handful of these birds make it across to the UK. The Stover Sora was only the thirteenth record for Britain and the first for nine years.

We spent the night in a walker's hostel in Oakhampton and kept the drinking to a minimum. After a quick early breakfast, we made our way towards Dartmoor. A quick stop at Burrator Reservoir was rewarded by views of a smart drake Ring-necked Duck. After a scenic drive south, we arrived at the very pretty village of East Prawle.

This village acts as the gateway to the birder's hotspot of Prawle Point. Our group got a little fragmented as we walked along the path towards Prawle Point, where we hoped to find some Cirl Bunting. Those of us that were a bit slower were treated to views of the most exciting bird of the trip. There had been a couple of buzzards passing overhead that caught our attention briefly. Then I located another raptor that I initially thought was going to be another pale buzzard. However, there was something very different about this bird. Although this raptor was similar in size to a Common Buzzard its flight profile was distinctly different. It held its wings much flatter when soaring. We could also notice the pale 'landing lights' on its shoulders. It was then I knew we were watching something special. As the bird glided overhead, we could see the contrast from the pale almost white underside and underwing coverts that contrasted dramatically with the dark secondaries, primaries, and its square edged tail. We were in no doubt that we were in the presence of a pale-phase Booted Eagle, an absolute mega encounter. I think it's fair to assume that this was a brief relocation of the bird that had recently been seen in Cornwall.

After all the excitement we joined the rest of our group who were already enjoying nice views of a singing Cirl Bunting. This was a fitting end to what had been a successful and unquestionably monumental birding trip to south-western England. Despite Kath not being a birder, she quite enjoyed the adventure!

With our two girls keeping us occupied and grounded, Kath and I decided to take them on holiday to Cornwall in the autumn. We were staying in a static caravan at St Buryan. The inevitable birding started in West Yorkshire at Featherstone on our way south. I was hoping to see a Laughing Gull that had been present for a few days. This Nearctic gull was hot on my wants list, but they had been difficult to come by in during the early to mid-2000's. We connected with the bird quite quickly, which was a fantastic start to the holiday.

We arrived in St Buryan and settled ourselves into the accommodation. I knew there had been a Blackpoll Warbler at Lower Moors on Scilly for some time, so after a bit of family negotiation the plan was for me to daytrip the islands the following morning.

My mode of transport this time was the helicopter. I did not enjoy the big noisy bus-like aircraft, but it got me to where I wanted to be. There were quite a few twitchers that had travelled to St Mary's that morning, not for the long staying Blackpoll Warbler, but for the Chimney Swift found the previous day. Because I had previously seen a Chimney Swift at Spurn, my plan was to go straight to Lower Moors in the hope of seeing the Nearctic warbler. I knew I could always see the swift later if it was available.

Arriving at Lower Moors, I was astonished to see that I was the only birder present. This was nice as it meant I had the opportunity to locate the Blackpoll Warbler myself. It did not take long before I was enjoying fantastic views of the target bird, my first American warbler. Nearby I got nice views of a Sora, only my second sighting of this rare American rail. Soon after that I had brief views of what turned out to be a very elusive 'un-streaked *acro*' (a type of Reed Warbler). After a few hours of painstaking patience, I got decisive views of the bird and, after studying all the salient features, I was able to identify it as my first ever observation of the rare Blyth's Reed Warbler. This would have made the trip worthwhile by itself. That daytrip had in paid dividends; it was good to get back to my family at the caravan though.

The following days we spent our time sightseeing, visiting family and, of course, birding. Despite our visit being in early November, the birding was very special. Visits to sites like Marazion Marsh, the Lizard, Sennon, Drift, the Hayle Estuary and Nanquidno Valley gave us a nice array of species like my second ever Franklin's Gull, Grey Phalarope, American Wigeon, Long-billed-Dowitcher Spoonbill, Green-winged Teal and Dartford Warbler. Not a bad little haul! Remember that Laughing Gull we detoured for on our way south, in Yorkshire? Well, things were going to get a bit interesting. There was a small influx of the species occurring. Firstly, there were two Laughing Gulls of different ages at Penzance, then a further two in the Nanquidno Valley. This was amazing. Five different Laughing Gulls in a week was astonishing. The girls really enjoyed the holiday, and I was happy that they got to meet some of my family at least.

On what we expected to be the last day of our holiday, news broke that a Solitary Sandpiper had been located on St Agnes. After securing an extra night in the caravan I was planning another day trip to the Isles of Scilly. This time my mode of transport was the Scillonian. This was preferrable to the chopper, despite it making for a longer day. Adding to the Laughing Gull influx tally, as I was leaving Hugh Town in the boat to St Agnes, I managed to see a further three Laughing Gulls, incredibly taking my week's tally up to eight individual birds. Once I had landed on St Agnes a local resident birder kindly took me and another couple down to see the

Solitary Sandpiper. The Nearctic wader was giving remarkably close views as it searched for food in the numerous puddles on the polythene sheeting in the small field it was frequenting.

On the way back in the dark I was sorry my girls were not with me, because it was November the fifth and I could see firework displays going on along the whole coastline, a magical sight. Having made it safely back to the caravan, we got a good night sleep before our journey home the following day. The Laughing Gull count was not quite over as there had been a further two located in Newquay. Given that I was already committed to this unprecedented influx, it would have been rude of me not to maximise my involvement. We spent a bit of time at Newquay boating ponds and enjoyed fantastic views of what were my ninth and tenth Laughing Gulls of the week! We'd had a fantastic holiday, but as is usually the case, it was nice to get back to our own home again.

The incredibly confiding juvenile Steppe Grey Shrike at
Grainthorpe Haven in Lincolnshire

Solitary Sandpiper on St Agnes, Isles of Scilly

Desert Wheatear at Bempton Cliffs in Yorkshire

Hoopoe at Carsethorn in Dumfries & Galloway

Bonaparte's Gull at Larne

Juvenile Masked Shrike at Kilnsea

Female Hooded Merganser at Tayport in Fife

American Buff-bellied Pipit at Burton Marsh in Cheshire

Marsh Fritillary

Adonis Blue

Purple Emperor

Duke of Bergundy

Red-veined Darter

Yellow-winged Darter

Blue-eyed Hawker

Broad-bodied Chaser

Act Three
Birding Globe

The natural progression from birding trips in Britain and Ireland, was of course visiting continental Europe. After a bit of planning and organisation by Derek, we were soon on our way to Alicante in Southern Spain. This was my first birding trip to mainland Europe. I was extremely excited with what we were likely to see, this was of course my biggest wildlife adventure to date.

We were in southern Spain in July, so the temperature was regularly hitting 40 degrees Celsius (104 degrees Fahrenheit), this would take some getting used to. We drank a lot of water throughout the days and that helped a lot! Although I certainly was not used to it, I really enjoyed the heat.

We began our birding at some saltpans not from Alicante. The first birds we could not ignore were a small group of Greater Flamingos. Now, if you do not get excited about these ridiculous pink iconic birds then may I suggest that you're looking in the wrong direction! Of course, I may have been more excited than most! At the first job I had back in my mid-teens working as a keeper at Paradise Park, one of the many species we were tasked with caring for was a colony of Chilean Flamingos. Okay, so the birds we were enjoying on the saltpans were a different species, but it was still fantastic to see these ungainly pink weirdos in a wild setting.

Some other familiar species such as Avocet, Black-winged Stilt, Kentish Plover and Yellow-legged Gull added to the experience as did my first ever Slender-billed Gull. This was a very nice start to the trip. We also visited an interesting bit of lumpy, scrubby, grassy habitat with a small wetland area. This turned out to be rich in some very interesting birdlife.

Quite early on, we had seen both Iberian Shrike and Iberian Green Woodpecker, two birds that were high on my wants list. Things continued in this vein as we explored the site. Additional highlights were Black Wheatear, Western Black-eared Wheatear, Blue Rock Thrush, Booted Eagle, Marbled Duck, and the 'giant blue chicken,' the Purple Swamphen (also referred to as Purple Gallinule). This was a strong start! We were staying in a beautiful small town called Oliva. The flat was owned by a friend of Derek's, Jules Sykes. Jules was great, he worked as a wildlife tour guide both in Spain and further afield. We had booked him for a few days guiding later in the week.

That evening we just chilled on the roof terrace, with an eye overlooking the orange grove. This wasn't overly productive, although we did see our first Spotless Starlings. The following days we spent time exploring some of the local marshes and wetlands and any nearby interesting habitats. It was amazing! Lots of high calibre birds were observed. My rather lengthy list of personal highlights included Squacco Heron, Purple Heron, Night Heron, Cattle Egret, Gull-billed Tern, Whiskered Tern, Collared Pratincole, Sardinian Warbler, Zitting Cisticola and Crested Lark. These were all special to see, but my personal highlight came during a nocturnal visit to the marshes. The bird we were looking at was the Red-necked Nightjar. The nightjars would spend time hawking for insects over the marshes, interspersed by time perched on the access tracks. The tracks were still warm from the heat of the sun and offered the birds some welcome heat. This was an incredible experience! We managed amazing views, and I even got some images with my quite new DSLR camera. Spain had already exceeded my expectations.

The first day that Jules put his wildlife guide hat on he took us to an area of steppe habitat. This is quite a rare habitat in Europe and an ecotype that I'd never seen before. Here we saw a fantastic range of interesting species such as Great Bustard, Little Bustard, Black-bellied Sandgrouse, Montagu's Harrier, Short-toed Snake Eagle and Lesser Short-toed Lark. At some nearby sites we also saw Greater Short-toed Lark, Roller, Rock Bunting, Alpine Swift, and Crag Martin.

It wasn't just about the birds of course as we also encountered Moorish Gecko, Iberian Grass Snake and Viperine Snake on the reptile front, and butterfly species such as Scarce Swallowtail, Black Satyr, Dusky Heath and Pale Clouded Yellow. Dragonflies were also in evidence and some of the highlights were Broad Scarlet and Long Skimmer. Another invertebrate that was in evidence everywhere we went, was the very vocal *Cicada barbara*, these cicadas were usually heard only as they were very tricky to locate. Fortunately, we did manage to get close views of one individual.

The following days we spent much of our time at a finca hosted by a couple of former UK residents. This was a site that was usually very reliable for Bonelli's Eagle. Unfortunately, the eagles did not appear for us. Not all was negative, though, as it was good to see Thekla Lark and Subalpine Warbler. We also spent a surprising amount of time trying to entice tarantulas out of their burrows! The rest of the trip was spent searching interesting habitats to see what we could find. We did well with Great Spotted Cuckoo and perhaps surprising a Red-necked Phalarope. The trip had been an amazing success with fantastic birds and other wildlife seen.

Red-necked Nightjar

Turtle Dove

Viperine Snake

Moorish Gecko

Broad Scarlet

Long Skimmer

Following our Spanish trip, we began organising our next adventure. I'd been in touch with Derek and Chris, and we had collectively decided that our next overseas birding adventure would take us to Türkiye. This was very exciting.

I'd recently been diagnosed with severe sleep apnoea. This is a disorder that means I stop breathing for several minutes at a time, numerous times a night whilst asleep. People with unmanaged sleep apnoea are not permitted to drive just in case they cause an accident by falling asleep at the wheel. So, it didn't look like I would be driving anytime soon.

Given I would not be able to contribute to our planned Anatolian trip by sharing the driving duties I offered to take a lead in the planning of the holiday. We curated a list of target species, and it was definitely an exciting list. I spent a lot of time trawling through trip reports and guidebooks and produced an itinerary that I was both proud and excited about. I also booked a guide for a couple of days that would give better chance of seeing some of the high mountain species. I really enjoyed the planning process and it helped reduce my depressive symptoms for a while.

The day of our flight to Türkiye soon arrived and we were all super excited for what the following ten days would bring. Because Türkiye straddles Europe and Asia it has a rich range of habitats that are host to a huge diversity of birds. A proportion of the birds we would see would be quite familiar to us, though a lot would be less so. The three of us from Cumbria and Dumfries and Galloway landed into Istanbul and awaited Derek's arrival. Having picked up our hire car it was birding time. Okay, so this is not a trip report as such, but I do want to share some of my incredible highlights from the adventure with you. Türkiye was a vastly different experience compared to Spain, but I had no idea that it would end up changing the course of my life, possibly for the better.

Our first experience of birding in Türkiye was to Tuzla Gölü. We saw some interesting waders like Spur-winged Plovers, Kentish Plovers, and Broad-billed Sandpipers. All exciting species, though Spur-winged Plovers became less so as they seemed to be pretty much everywhere we went! Surprisingly, there were very few gulls present, Slender-billed Gull was the only gull species we recorded there. Looking at passerines (perching and songbirds) was where it got interesting.

The first species of passerines that we saw was the very pretty Graceful Prinia. This was high on my wants list, so it was fantastic to see one so early on in the trip. Next, we saw the strikingly stunning White-throated Robin. This was an extremely exciting find for everyone. Things were getting interesting when we found not one, but fifteen Thrush Nightingales in quite a small area. It was clear that there had been a 'fall' of migrants on this land mass. A fall in this context is a term used to describe a situation where weather conditions align with numbers of migratory birds and dumps them on a headland or similar. This was an amazing start to our visit, but our next habitat step-up would be monumental. This was the part of the trip that I'd booked a guide for, as we were heading into the Taurus mountains near the Aladağ massive not far from Çamardı.

Before we met our guide, we decided to explore the narrow gorge near to Demirkazik ski centre. It was incredible! We hadn't got to the gorge proper, and we were watching the iconic Red-fronted Serin, a species I'd been aware of since I was a child, but never dreamt I would ever see. Next up was Crag Martin's flying overhead and then a magnificent Rock Thrush singing from a cliff face. Western Rock Nuthatch was also a superb bird to see.

The top prize however went to, not one, not two, but if memory serves me correctly, five mythical Wallcreepers showing nicely in various areas of the gorge walls. I think these striking small grey birds with crimson wings and long gently curved beaks stand above the foray because they look so unlike any other species. They are impressive, though, I can vouch for that. It was soon time for us to make our way to our accommodation and meet our guide Başar Şafak. We were staying in Özşafak Pension, which was owned and managed by Başar and his family.

After enjoying a very nice evening meal and going outside to hear a very vocal Scops Owl, we went to bed to catch an early night's sleep. We had been told that there was a bad weather system approaching, so it was unlikely that we would be able to get up into the mountains. This was disappointing, but to our surprise we got a wake-up call at around two-thirty in the morning and we were informed that conditions were better than expected.

I had spent a lot of time watching or surveying birds in the British uplands, but this would be the first proper mountain birding experience I'd ever had. I was excited, nervous, and anxious all rolled into one. None of us had slept particularly well, but I think the anticipation of where we were going, kept us energised. We jumped into our hire car and made the short trip to the mountain trailhead. Here we met our transport and driver that would take us up into the mountains.

Our transport was one of those old, vintage, cab-less tractors, not what I was expecting to be honest! Our group and Başar clambered aboard, I am not sure how we found space for six grown men, but we did. I was perched on the arch of the left-hand rear wheel, a precarious position, I gripped on very tightly. It was not until the return journey in daylight that I realised how good it was that we travelled up in the pitch black. There were some very scary drops on my side of the tractor, thankfully I was not aware of them at the time.

The journey up was very bumpy to say the least, the track was muddy in places and rocky throughout as you'd expect. It was beginning to get light when we arrived at the snowline. We disembarked here and began the walk to the Arpalık plateau that sits at an impressive height of around 7,200 ft (2,200 m) above sea level. Early on in our walk we could already hear some Caspian Snowcocks calling, this did bode very well. The light was fairly good when we reached the plateau, the views were breathtaking. We set our optics up and started scanning the ridge line above us.

The first sighting was a mammal, some Bezoar Ibex, a subspecies of wild goat. Soon we were getting decent views of our main target species here, the Caspian Snowcock. These are incredible looking birds, looking like a huge grey and white partridge. Snowcocks tend to go quiet by about nine in the morning and this was the case on our visit. It was a nice opportunity to walk around the plateau to see if we could find any other mountain specialities. We managed views of a *libanitica* Northern Wheatear, a *bella* Linnet and a *breviirostris* Twite. Some very interesting subspecies. The birding quality was on an upward curve when we saw at least four Wallcreepers flying overhead as well as another singing Rock Thrush. The mountain specialities then came thick and fast with amazing views of Alpine Chough, Radde's Accentor, Alpine Accentor, Asian Crimson-winged Finch and White-winged Snowfinch. Back along the mountain track we saw a lot of Eastern Black-eared Wheatear, Chukar and a Finsch's Wheatear. My first experience mountain birding was simply incredible. Not only had we seen some impressive and exciting birds, but our host and guide Başar had been amazing.

We stopped off at a few sites that Başar had given us directions and information for, and saw some stunning birds such as Cinereous Bunting, Ortolan Bunting, Cretzschmar's Bunting, Greater Short-toed Lark, Lesser Short-toed Lark, Calandra Lark, Bimaculated Lark and Sombre Tit. Türkiye was incredible! We spent a few days travelling southeast towards Birecik. The birding highlights were Black Kites, Booted Eagles, Eleonora's Falcon, Saker Falcon,

Laughing Dove, Syrian Woodpeckers, Lesser Spotted Woodpecker, Black-capped Jay, Woodchat Shrike, Crested Lark, Rüppell's Warbler, Krüper's Nuthatch, White-throated Robin, Spanish Sparrow, Citrine Wagtail, Corn Bunting and Black-headed Bunting. Durnalik is situated just to the northeast of Gaziantep and has some great areas for birds. We explored an interesting little valley, and it was very interesting. The highlights there were Asian Long-legged Buzzard, Sombre Tit, another White-throated Robin, Blue Rock Thrush, and an Eastern Rock Nuthatch on a massive nest.

We arrived in Birecik late afternoon during a thunderstorm, but we still managed views of Pygmy Cormorants, Little Swifts and Northern Bald Ibis before we checked into our accommodation. At the time of our visit Northern Bald Ibis were classified by the International Union for the Conservation of Nature (IUCN) as critically endangered. There were only two populations known globally (the Birecik population and another small population in northern Morocco).

When it was realised, the species was in in real danger of extinction, the Türkiye government took a major and perhaps controversial step. They built enclosures near to the breeding cliffs and in late summer/early autumn when the young had fledged, the Ibis are ushered into the pens where they would spend the winter. The purpose of this drastic action was to prevent the birds from migrating southwards through Syria and beyond, where they would be in real danger of being hunted.

We spent a fair bit of time at the Northern Bald Ibis Centre, drinking tea and chatting to Mustafa, the bird's guardian. Mustafa was fantastic! He was so happy to talk to us and he also give us advice on some nearby birding hot spots. The Northern Bald Ibis could be considered an acquired taste, because they do not necessarily have classical good looks like a Wallcreeper does. I have a soft spot for them, they are so distinctive and charismatic.

In my younger years when I worked in the Cornish bird zoo, I looked after a small colony; I knew them as Waldrap Ibis back then. With the work that has been continued by Mustafa and a successful reintroduction project in Spain and Morocco the IUCN status has been downgraded to endangered. This is good news, although they are still far from out of the woods yet.

One of our target species for this area was See-See Partridge, having failed to find any at our researched site we asked Mustafa for some help. He gave us information on a site a little distance away. Despite his directions we failed to find the place on two attempts. Mustafa agreed to guide us onto the site. This involved following him on his moped. Thankfully, on arrival at the spot, we were soon enjoying views of our first See-See Partridge. As a bonus we also had nice views of a pair of Desert Finches. Mustafa, what an absolute legend!

On our way back to Birecik, we decided to take a slight detour to explore some interesting habitat. This turned out not to be our most sensible decision as we found ourselves a bit too close to a military area. This soon saw us confronted by soldiers. One of them stood in front of our car pointing his gun at us, whilst another attempted to interrogate us. He did not speak English and we didn't speak Turkish, so communication was very challenging. However, once we showed him the images on our camera, we were thankfully free to go. That was a close one that could have gone very differently!

We spent a good few days exploring habitats in the Birecik area. From wetland sites like gravel pits and the banks of the Euphrates to some arid semi-desert wadis. We saw a lot of very high-class birds. My highlights were Pygmy Cormorant, Baltic Gull, Armenian Gull, Pied Kingfisher, Smyrna Kingfisher, Pallid Scops Owl, Lilith's Owl, Black Francolin, Roller, Lesser Grey Shrike, Rufous-tailed Scrub Robin, Iraq Babbler, Isabelline Wheatear, Eastern Olivaceous Warbler, Upcher's Warbler, Eastern Orphean

Warbler, Menetries's Warbler, Rock Sparrow, Dead sea Sparrow, Pale Rock Sparrow, Chestnut-shouldered Petronia, and Rock Bunting. After a successful visit to Işıklı, near Gaziantep, to see Kurdish Wheatear we made our way west for the remainder of our trip.

We visited a variety of sites, but the best was the Göksu Delta. The highlights from this portion of the trip were, White Pelican, Marsh Sandpiper, Audouin's Gull Caspian Tern, Marbled Duck, Grey-headed Swamphen, Masked Shrike, Moustached Warbler, White-spectacled Bulbul, and Black- headed Wagtail. It wasn't just about the birds either; Spur-thighed Tortoise, Southern White-breasted Hedgehog, Andalusian Ground Squirrel and Egyptian Mongoose were all particularly impressive.

We'd had an absolutely incredible trip, amazing bird after amazing bird and we'd met some beautiful people. It was going to take a while for the gravity of this intense experience to sink in. I had struggled a little bit with my mental health whilst away, but the distraction of great wildlife, stunning scenery and incredible people had insured that it did not get out of control. In fact, on my return home, my mood was extremely high. It had been an amazing trip, although it was nice to be back home. I was excited to tell Kathleen and the kids about my adventures.

Northern Bald Ibis in Birecik

Little or Byzantine Owl near to Birecik

European Roller near Birecik

Ortolan Bunting near to Çamardı

Martin Garner had set up his birding community that he had named Birding Frontiers. When Chris and I heard that he had got a gull identification workshop planned at Saltholme Pools RSPB reserve, we got ourselves booked on. This was a no brainer!

The workshop was fantastic. Martin was always incredibly engaging and shared his knowledge in a clear and inclusive way. Aside from the educational side of things, the day was a nice opportunity to meet up with friends and other like-minded people.

After the workshop finished, I got chatting with Martin about birding stuff and a unique conservation project on which I was working. He told me about a trip he was involved with in the following year for a new wildlife festival in Arctic Norway, called Gullfest. He then went on to suggest that I should be going too. I am not sure what Martin saw in me, but whatever it was I am incredibly grateful.

After a few phone calls by Martin and a bit of toing and froing with emails, I had been invited to join Martin in Arctic Norway for the inaugural Gullfest. This was huge, a country I never envisaged I would go to, and my first opportunity to give a talk to an international audience. I was nervous and excited! I was really looking forward to the adventure, although I still couldn't quite understand how I was seen as interesting enough to be invited out to participate in this intriguing new wildlife festival in the Arctic.

I had my freezing weather kit, my binoculars, my telescope, and my camera. I was ready for my trip northwards. After flying into arctic Norway, I met up with organisers Tormod, Elin, Martin and Sharon along with other attendees Ian Wright, Seamus Enright, Vincent van der Spek, Murray Yeomans, Nils van Duivendijk, Willem Visser, Mike Robinson.

I already knew Mike as he lived in the south of Cumbria, and we had birded together on many an occasion, as well as travelled to see scarce wildlife in various corners of the UK. I knew Nils only really by his online presence and his body of work as one of the greatest minds in western Palearctic bird identification. I did not know it at the time, but Vincent would take an important role in trying to reduce my life expectancy by crashing me into multiple trees in the taiga forest! As for the others, I was very much looking forward to getting to know them.

Although this was merely the prologue to Gullfest, it certainly was a creative and dramatic start to our adventure. We arrived in the Pasvik on the Finnmark massive. It was dark when we got to the Birk Husky Guesthouse near Melkefossveien, but this added to the drama of our introduction to the area. As soon as we arrived, we were directed into their amazingly atmospheric Viking longhouse restaurant. The fires were roaring along the length of the room giving the atmosphere the right mix of cosy and drama. Our host, Trine and her team made us feel very welcome. The food was great, though I do not think they were anticipating a vegetarian. Nevertheless, I was catered for brilliantly. The group really seemed to get on well, so I was really looking forward to the days ahead.

I woke up early the following morning and although I tried hard to keep things buried, my depression was starting to rear its ugly head again. I was very overwhelmed with things and imposter syndrome was in the forefront. This was most likely the trigger. I decided to try a walk to see if that helped settle my mind. The snowy scenery was simply stunning, and I lucked in with views of my first Pine Grosbeak, Siberian Jay, and Willow Ptarmigan of the trip. This was a necessary diversion to help me keep more positive.

After a great Norwegian breakfast (avoiding the Fløtemysost), we got kitted out in the provided thermal gear and then we got to meet our gorgeous husky team. After introducing ourselves to the dogs, we tethered them up ready for our dog sled trip into the forest.

There were two humans per dog sled, and I teamed up with my new Dutch friend, Vincent.

Taiga forest, also referred to as boreal forest, is considered as earth's largest biome. The dominant trees in the sub-arctic habitat are spruce, birch and larch. This felt like real wilderness habitat. Exploring by dog sled certainly seemed to be the only way to experience this habitat. In Vincent's defence, we were in the Pasvik in spring, so the snow was softer than would be ideal. Vincent was keen to drive the sled and I was keen not to, so it was a perfect partnership! If memory serves me correctly, we all had about fifteen kilometres to cover before we arrived at the bird cabin.

It was an eventful journey through beautiful landscape with frequent stops to pull my teeth out of the taiga tree trunks! My first experience of dog sledding was awesome! As we secured the huskies at the cabin, someone from the group had found a Northern Hawk Owl. This iconic species was high on my list of birds I had always hoped I would see. It was an extremely exciting moment.

Despite being a distance away, its distinctive shape made it easily recognisable. This species of owl is diurnal, active during the day. It turned out Tormod had a very crowd-pleasing trick up his sleeve, in the form of a lure. The lure was deployed onto the snow, to mimic a mouse or vole. Instantaneously the Hawk Owl had locked on to it and was flying at speed towards us. The views were point blank incredible!

The bird feeding area next to the cabin were also continually active. We managed amazing views of Pine Grosbeaks, Siberian Jays, borealis Willow Tits and Siberian Tits. An amazing collection of taiga specialists. After making it back to the guest house, we had a nice meal and discussed what an astonishing start to our arctic adventure we had experienced.

The following morning, we boarded the Hurtigruten for our journey to Vardø further up the Varangar Fjord. Unsurprisingly we spent a sizeable portion of the boat journey on the deck in awe of the dramatic scenery and searching for birdlife. We certainly were not disappointed as, by the time we reached land again, we'd seen Common Eider, King Eider, Steller's Eider, and Brünnich's Guillemot. Incredibly as we passed the seabird cliffs of Hørnoya, we watched a Gyr Falcon as it worked the auk colonies in search of prey.

We disembarked the Hurtigruten and made our way to the Vardø Hotel, where we were based during the festival. I could not believe my eyes when I looked out my room window! There was a small group of Steller's Eider loafing remarkably close by in the harbour. The Steller's Eider was a species that I had dreamt of seeing since I was a child. I remember being captivated by illustrations of the species in my bird identification field guide, so getting such amazing views of these charismatic ducks was really special.

After a delicious evening meal at the hotel, we made our way to the North Pole pub for the official opening of Gullfest. Tormod and Martin each gave inspiring talks in their very different engaging styles. Tormod is an interesting guy; he is an architect that specialises in bringing nature to people in the most sustainable way possible. He had Incredible enthusiasm for Varangar, and it was my understanding that the festival was not only to highlight the area as a birding and wildlife destination, but also to illustrate to the local community that this type of tourism could be a good source of sustainable income. It was a very good showcase.

In the following days I got to explore the nearby environs, the island of Hørnoya, and an interesting pelagic into the Barents Sea. Some of the highlights were, arctic Guillemots, Brünnich's Guillemots, Atlantic Puffins, Razorbills, Shags, Glaucous Gulls, Long-tailed Ducks, King Eiders, Steller's Eiders, Rough-legged Buzzards, Reindeer, and the ubiquitous Snow Buntings. Each day was underlined with great hospitality and some fantastic talks from some very impressive people on subjects ranging from wildlife conservation to shiny new behavioural studies and cutting-edge bird identification. Although imposter syndrome was at the forefront of my mind, I nervously delivered my quite different talk about my Turkish conservation project. I am pleased to say, it was well received. In this case, different was good! The Gullfest proper had now finished, but our group and some of the other attendees still had the Gullfest epilogue!

We headed onto the mainland and made our way down the coast to Vadsø. Stopping at one of the harbours, Tormod and his team put down some of the remaining fish to see what gulls we could attract in: big numbers of Scandinavian Herring Gulls (including a few intriguing individuals with yellow legs) and a handful of Glaucous Gulls. In the harbour there were good numbers of Steller's Eider along with smaller numbers of Common Eider. En route to Vadsø we clocked a few White-tailed Eagles, Yellow-billed Divers, King Eiders, Steller's Eiders and scoters.

We then met up with Arntzen before travelling into the taiga on skidoos! On arrival, we enjoyed a barbeque lunch, fantastic close views of Siberian Tit and point-blank views of Coues's Arctic Redpolls. Nearby we were treated to more views of Northern Hawk Owls, including a pair visiting a nest box. However, the biggest surprise was fabulous views of a Tengmalm's Owl! This was a species none of us expected to see.

A few of our group had a bonus day of birding after the event had closed. After managing views of Willow Grouse and Snow Hare, we decided to explore the Tana Valley. What a beautiful area it was! Along the taiga sections of the valley, we observed an astounding eight Northern Hawk Owls and as we climbed up into the tundra habitat, we all fell silent in awe of the majestic and vast landscape. The final bonus, and my wildlife highlight, was getting amazing views of a Norwegian Lemming. For me Arctic Norway had been an incredible experience. The wildlife and the scenery had been breathtaking and the people, both local and visiting, had really made the trip even more special. This was a trip that I would remember for a very long time.

It was fantastic birding and chatting with Martin and Sharon, they had a lovely caring dominant component to their personalities, they always made me feel welcome and valued. I knew that both were practicing Christian's, they were very much free spirits and would describe themselves as spiritual rather than religious. My personal view on religion was vastly different to theirs. Despite being raised as a Christian, time, trauma and too many unanswered questions had made me an agnostic atheist. I liked the fact that Martin and Sharon respected my opinions e. Having returned home it was great to see Kathleen and the kids and show them some pictures of the scenery, people, birds, and mammals I encountered.

Coues's Arctic Redpoll

Siberian Tit

Pine Grosbeak

Northern Hawk Owl

Steller's Eiders

Norwegian Lemming

I was still enjoying some local birding with Chris, with regular trips further afield when required. Accessible rarities seemed a little sparse during 2012, but we did connect with a few nice species like a couple of Desert Wheatears, Western Sandpiper, Olive-backed Pipit, Eastern Olivaceous Warbler and Radde's Warbler. One of the most notable twitches during this period was when we went to see a Thayer's Gull in Lincolnshire. This was only a short time after our visit to Enniskillen for the same gull subspecies, so it was useful to have identification knowledge fresh in our minds. What was even better than that was bumping into Martin onsite. It was incredible to be able to discuss identification details with him whilst watching the Thayer's Gull. It was always a pleasure to chat to Martin, so this catch up was perfectly timed.

Martin had really developed his Birding Frontiers brand and his exciting website dedicated to advanced bird identification was going from strength to strength. Martin had assembled a Birding Frontiers team of high calibre pioneers in the field of bird identification, including such luminaries as Dani López-Velasco, Chris Gibbins, Tormod Amundsen, Roger Riddington, Nils van Duivendijk, Yoav Perlman, Sam Jones, Paul Lehman, Terry Townshend, Tony Davidson, Jochen Dierschke, José Luis Copete, Andrea Corso and Steve Blain. This list of names features a broad selection of world class, pioneering experts in bird identification, bird research, bird conservation and bird photography. These people. Along with Martin, were really pushing the frontier of our understanding of birding, particularly, but not confined to, the geographical region referred to as the western Palearctic. Here is the curve ball though, the team member I haven't mentioned is me.

To this day, I have no idea why Martin invited me to join his Birding Frontiers team. For context, although I could be accused of having a passion for increasing my bird identification knowledge, there was no practical evidence that I had become an expert or a specialist in any corner of this niche. I really was a half-arsed jack of all trades and master of none. That's my wheelhouse! Whatever Martin thought he saw in me that he believed would add value to his extraordinarily talented team, I am forever grateful. The opportunity to gain experience, meet amazing people and feel valued for perhaps the first time in my life, would not have happened without Martin.

Following on from the early spring visit to arctic Norway, thanks to Martin, I was invited out to the late autumn, Hula Bird Festival in Israel. I was excited about this as Israel is a very special place for birds and bird migration. Travelling to Israel does of course court some controversy, given the political situation. Because of this, there are a lot of people who believe that we should all boycott Israel. Of course, I understand this standpoint, but I do not believe that this protest is particularly fair in most cases. My thoughts are that boycotting is a form of protest that requires no real effort, it is lazy activism. Sometimes you need to look deeper into things and depolarise the view. I put things into context in my mind, by looking at my country, its history and its present. What I concluded was that I would not find it fair to be blamed for the atrocities (both physical and economic) conducted by those in charge. There are a lot of good people in the world, who would not and do not support or condone the horrible decisions made by their governments. So, you know, that, and birds!

I flew out to Tel Aviv with Martin, full of excited anticipation for this festival. I was not required to give a talk. I was there more as a journalist, well an online journalist! Going through security was interesting, being asked the same set of questions at several random points throughout the airport. My letter from the Israeli Ministry of Tourism did not seem to help, although I was sporting a Mohawk and a head tattoo! Once we got through security, we grabbed a coffee and awaited Birding Frontiers team member,

Yoav, who was hosting us. I noticed signs requesting people did not bring weapons into the building, this was a quite different country than I was used to.

Yoav soon arrived and we were on our way to experience our first few hours of birding in Israel. We visited some sites in the Negev. It was interesting to see an *ochuros* Black Redstart, the same subspecies I'd seen in Türkiye. It was also good to see Graceful Prinia again. My first new birds of the trip were the stunningly shiny Palestinian Sunbird, the Mourning Wheatear, the White-crowned Black Wheatear and one of my all-time favourites, the Blackstart. Perhaps the highlight of the afternoon were incredible views of a small family group of Nubian Ibex. Certainly, a very nice start to the trip. We ended the day with a nice meal with Yoav and his family, learning a little about Israeli culture.

The following morning, we were in the Negev Desert for some top-quality birding. I really love desert birding! During this visit, the highlights for me were Rock Martin, Scrub Warbler and more Mourning Wheatears. We also spent some time at Ashdod with Yoav and Amir, where I had a very intense gull identification education masterclass. We saw Armenian Gulls, Heuglien's Gulls, Baltic Gulls, Caspian Gulls, Yellow-legged Gulls and Steppe Gulls.

It was an interesting few hours learning from the experts. We also visited the fishponds at Ma'agan Michael, this was also productive for gulls, with a similar haul to Ashdod. We also saw Purple Herons, Great Egret, Little Egret and Night Heron, Hoopoe and the three kingfisher species. We also had nice views of an Egyptian Mongoose. We drove up to the Hula Valley and did a quick tour of the reserve. This was a real taster of what was to come during the festival. Some of the highlights were Oriental Turtle Dove, White Pelicans, Pygmy Cormorants, Greater Flamingos, Greater Spotted Eagles, Booted Eagles, Marsh Harriers, Montagu's Harrier, Moustached Warbler and incredibly a huge Wild Boar. What a place! During the evening, the official opening of the festival was activated with some fascinating talks by Yoav, Dan, Jonathan, and Martin.

The following morning, we were up early for the sunrise tractor tour. Being in amongst an estimated 35,000 very vocal and dancing cranes was incredible! One of the most amazing wildlife encounters of my life. In addition to the cranes, we had magnificent views of a mammal species I was not expecting, a Jungle Cat! Exploring the surrounding areas throughout the day produced White Pelicans, Marbled Ducks, White-tailed Eagles, Greater Spotted Eagles, Eastern Imperial Eagles, Pallid Harrier, Black Kites, Asian Black-shouldered Kites, Merlins, Citrine Wagtails, Red-throated Pipits, Palestinian Sunbirds, European Kingfishers, Smyrna Kingfisher and Pied Kingfisher. The kingfishers really do illustrate why Israel is well placed to attract a vast range of migrant birds. The European Kingfisher, as its name suggests, is predominantly a European species, the Smyrna Kingfisher is predominantly an Asian species, and the Pied Kingfisher is predominantly an African species. Those three continents border Israel.

During the week, we visited some interesting sites such as Mount Herman, Golan Heights, Gamla, the Bet She'an Valley, Sea of Galilee and Neve Eitan fishponds. Some of the many bird highlights were Caspian Tern, Spur-winged Plovers, Greater Spotted Eagles, Pallid Harrier, Barbary Falcon, Eurasian Eagle Owl, Black Francolin, Arabian Babblers, Finsch's Wheatears, Little Swifts, Sinai Desert Larks, Long-billed Pipit, Clamorous Reed Warbler, Sombre Tit, Dead sea Sparrows, Desert Finches, Syrian Serin, Red-fronted Serin and Rock Sparrow. Those are just the ones I can remember all these years later! The mammal highlights, although not as many species, were still very high quality. We had several more sightings of Jungle Cats and Wild Boar, as well as observations of Mountain Gazelle, the ever-present feral Coypu's, Syrian Rock Hyrax, Desert Hare and Golden Jackal. The reptile highlight for me were the very impressive Starred Agama.

There were two species groups that really caught my attention during my visit. The first were the Siberian-type stonechats. This is a tricky group but, thankfully, I had one of birding's sharpest minds alongside to discuss and learn the finer points with. We spent an entire day searching for and studying these intriguing birds. During the day, we managed to see and identifying both Siberian Stonechat and Caspian Stonechat. It was a fantastic opportunity to really get to know these two taxa. The second group were my favourite group, the grey shrikes. There was huge opportunity to really study this group, with so many forms available. During the week, I was lucky enough to see Desert Grey Shrike, Asian Grey Shrike and my favourite, Arabian Grey Shrike. I was in my element!

Although I am an introvert that sometimes acts like an extrovert, I find interactions with new people quite a big challenge. I do like people though, and I really enjoyed the diversity of people's personalities and backgrounds and how that shapes them. There were such a range of humans that attended the festival, and I enjoyed spending time with these people. This really made the trip for me.

As the festival ended, Martin and I said our thanks and goodbyes before setting off for our last few days of birding. Jonathan took us to some nice wild habitats to the South, through the West Bank and on into Jerusalem. My personal highlights of that journey were seeing more of the now familiar Arabian Bee-eaters (formally known as Little Green Bee-eaters) and yet another few new species for me, the very striking Namaqua Dove and the slightly less striking, Brown-necked Raven. Jonathan dropped us in Jerusalem where we would spend the remaining days of our trip. Both Jonathan and Yoav had been fantastic hosts, guides, and friends during our visit, so it was quite emotional saying goodbye.

After checking into our accommodation, I suggested to Martin that we could have a walk into the old town and be tourists for a few hours. Martin said to me that he was not that bothered, but I sensed he may be just being polite given that he was already aware of my view on religion. Whatever the situation, I was sure Martin would enjoy the experience. After a bit of discussion, we started walking towards the old town. This was not me being selfless exactly. I might not agree with or understand modern religions, but I am fascinated by theology with a sociological perspective.

Besides, I had the Christian bible read to me regularly as a child and I have read it subsequently as an atheist adult, so, having already visited places in Israel like Mount Hermon, the Sea of Galilee and the Golan Heights I was certainly invested and interested to explore some of the historical parts of Jerusalem. Of course, we could not ignore birds during our walk into town, we enjoyed views of Israel's national bird, the Hoopoe. The old town was certainly fascinating, although I found it a little intense. There seemed to be a fair few religious ceremonies occurring in various rooms. I did not join Martin for most of them, because I felt my appearance (you know, shorts, t-shirt, mohawk, tattoos etc) may be perceived as disrespectful. Martin enjoyed his experiences. The following morning, we were up early as we were visiting the Nili and David Jerusalem Bird Observatory. Although this urban oasis sits between the Knesset and the supreme court, it has no direct political association as far as I am aware. It was set up by two ornithologists, Amir Balaban and Gidon Perlman to protect one of the most valuable bird migration habitats in the area. It has also developed into a place to study bird migration and a place to help educate people about birds and bird conservation.

It was certainly achieving these objectives during our visit. Avner Rinot, who hosted us at the observatory, was one of the most enthusiastic ornithologists I have ever had the pleasure to meet; his energy was infectious. We were witness to a ringing session, where I was extremely excited to get to see a Black-capped Jay in the hand, incredible! There were a lot of birds to see in the observatory grounds, with Smyrna Kingfisher, Hoopoe, Syrian Woodpecker,

Zitting Cisticola, Sardinian Warbler, and a good candidate Mountain Chiffchaff. Our final quality bird of the trip was a very striking juvenile Masked Shrike in the rose garden. A fitting finish to what had been a spectacular trip.

During my visit to Israel there was an escalation in violence between Hamas and Israel in Gaza. For me on the ground in Israel, I had no real concerns for my personal safety. My only real awareness of the situation, initially, was seeing some military mobilisation moving south on the roads. Kath however was more aware of the situation as there was a lot of coverage on the UK news. She was quite worried for me, but I never felt like I was in danger. I had been made aware that, at that time at least, after a resident had completed military service, they would then have to serve in the army reserves until they turned forty. This became a reality when my friend had to leave the festival promptly as he had been called up for military duty. After saying goodbye to him, I got quite emotional. I was deeply worried for his safety and what he might experience. Things got very real, very quickly. I am happy to tell you, that he is still actively pushing the boundaries of bird identification in the middle east and beyond.

What I learned from going to Israel was that holding a polarised view of a population of people because of the acts of their governments is both unfair and unhelpful. Go and meet the people, spend time with them and their families and try to look under the surface. What I found from meeting and engaging with many Israelis is that those I met were kind, welcoming and passionate people. I know people's opinions on the Israeli-Palestinian issues can be quite divisive, but I can only share with you my own experiences of the region. Excitingly. I saw how some engaged in very positive project where they used birds and bird migration as a tool to bring Palestinians and Israelis together. It was beautiful to see such positive things happening here despite the conflict. Wildlife and people can be a powerful force for good.

65

Blue Rock Thrush at Gamla

Steppe Gull at Ashdod

Eastern Imperial Eagle

Desert Shrike

Sinai Desert Lark in the Negev

Common Cranes in the Hula Valley

Nubian Ibex in the Negev

Jungle Cat in the Hula Valley

Syrian Rock Hyrax at Gamla

Starred Agama at Gamla

The great news for me was that I had been invited back to Vardø to participate in the second iteration of Gullfest. I did not join the prologue that year, so I went straight into Gullfest proper. It was a little stressful rendezvousing with the Hurtigruten this time as my flight was due to an unscheduled stop at Tromsø to de-ice the plane. However, thanks to Tormod negotiating with the captain, insisting that I was a VIP, and informing that it was imperative I made it to Vardø, the boat waited just long enough for me to jump on. Of course, I wasn't a VIP, I was just some nutter with a lot of bird tattoos!

The boat trip was a great mix of quality birding and catching up with folk. It was fantastic to see Tormod and Martin again, as well as a few familiar faces from the previous event, like Anders. It was also exciting to see friends Rob and Jonny were joining us for this epic experience, as well as Ian Lewington and Darren Woodhead, both top class pioneers in bird illustration and bird artwork.

Bird highlights on the mini voyage were the expected Guillemots, Razorbills, Puffins, Brünnich's Guillemots, Eiders, King Eiders and a small number of my favourites, Steller's Eiders. A genuinely nice and familiar start to the week. On arrival into Vardø it was really nice to see Elin again and I was happy to see that my old college friend, Rich, was there as part of the bird ringing contingent. For me, the wildlife highlights of the main festival were visiting the impressive Hørnoya bird cliffs for the usual suspects. Much to Rob and Jonny's delight we also had nice views of some Killer Whales. We also watched a Wren at the base of the sea cliffs, which we thought nothing of at the time. When I mentioned it to Tormod several days later, he nearly fell of his chair! Apparently, it is a rare species in that part of Norway.

Another highlight for me, was going out on a fishing boat for the King Eider safari. I'd been up late with Rob and Jonny, drinking too much whiskey and putting the world to rights. To say I was hungover the next morning was an understatement. So, rolling about on the Barents Sea in a big storm, seemed a great idea! The original plan was to visit Hørnoya seabird cliffs, but the stormy seas meant that we could not safely land on the island. Plan B was to go out into open seas to search for the King Eider flock. This turned out to be spectacular. We located a mega flock containing an estimated 8,500 Common Eider and a staggering 12,500 King Eider. Bearing in mind I had only seen around 10 King Eider over a few years in the UK and Ireland, this encounter was, well, emotional.

The massive flock would take flight on occasion and circle the boat, this is where I coined the phrase 'The King Eider Vortex.' This term seemed to catch on, I was quietly pleased with myself; even in my hungover state I could be a little bit creative! As a postscript to this event, when some photos taken of the vortex (not mine unfortunately) were studied, a striking drake Pacific Eider could be identified in the flock. This was the first European record of this taxon. A pity we all missed it on the day!

Gullfest 2013 was a lot bigger than the previous year, with attendees from at least ten different nations giving a fantastic international flavour. If you walk around Vardø you will notice a lot of high-quality bird and birding themed street art. The strong link between nature and art has been entertained for an age, but it was still amazing to see an art exhibition at the festival. There was an amazing array of art, not only from such icons as Ian Lewington and Darren Woodhead, but also from Skjalg Helmer Vian, a young enthusiastic and very talented wildlife photographer. During the week it was a real privilege to watch Ian and Darren create bind blowing art in their delectably unique styles. The talks were also of extremely high quality again in this second episode of Gullfest. Martin and Tormod gave amazing inspirational talks as I had come to expect. There was a range of fascinating talks about gull identification, gull science and gull evolution by both local and visiting ornithologists. Kate Utsi gave a captivating talk about life as a modern Sammi girl. I think I was in love with her by this stage!

Johan Anders Andersen gave us some culture with a Sammi folk song that included a lot of his personal interpretation of local bird calls. I am not sure how my talk stacked up against all that talent, but I was pleased to deliver it highlighting some innovative conservation projects like the Tattzoo Project. I was pleased to connect with the founder of the Tattzoo Project back home before Gullfest. It was great to share my tattoo project with her and her students. Tattzoo was a mentoring program where a student would learn about a species under threat and create a report on its conservation. When they graduated, they would get a tattoo of the species they were championing.

After Gullfest had finished, I joined the 'epilogue' group for a mini tour of northern Varanger. The main bird highlight was a hybrid boreal Willow Tit x Siberian Tit, Other highlights were White-tailed Eagle, grey phase Gyr Falcon, Coues's Arctic Redpoll, Reindeer and Moose. The visit to Båtsfjørd for the ingenious floating hides was fantastic. From the boat out to the hide we lucked in with a few Little Auk. The hide experience was amazing! We got incredibly close views of King Eiders, Steller's Eiders, Common Eiders, and Long-tailed Ducks. A high-class end to another incredible Gullfest in Arctic Norway. What a privilege.

Drake King Eider at Båtsfjørd

Drake King Eider at Båtsfjørd

Female King Eider at Båtsfjørd

Drake Steller's Eider at Båtsfjørd

After my trips to Türkiye and Israel and because of my fundraising initiative I became increasingly focused on birds and bird conservation, in the fascinating middle east region. When the opportunity surfaced, a natural progression was to become a trustee of OSME. OSME was formed in the 1970's and was originally known as the Ornithological Society of the Middle East. The purpose of the society is to record, collate and publish bird data of the region, encourage study and interest in birds and bird conservation within the region and support conservation and environmental organisations as well as nature societies in the middle east. Since 2001, the organisation broadened its geographic range to include the Caucasus and Central Asia. Although I felt out of my depth, I was immensely proud to be sitting on the committee of this very important organisation.

In my role as committee member, I made the trip down to Norfolk for the OSME summer meeting and AGM. This was a nice opportunity to catch up with Jonny and Rob who both lived down that way. Jonny kindly invited me to stay at his home over the weekend and we met up with Rob and Sven after the meeting.

We did a broad mix of birding and other interesting wildlife observations. For me, the highlights were Small Red Damselfly (the penultimate British *odonata* species I had left to see), and the very rare Fen Orchid. The meeting itself was really fascinating with some interesting and exciting talks about birds and bird conservation in the OSME region. For me personally, it was nice to get some positive feedback on how much awareness my 'giving my right arm' project was raising about the ecological disaster ongoing in Türkiye.

The only negative aspect to this trip was that I was missing Kathleen's first marathon, a trail marathon around Coniston Water. I knew her mother and twin sister would be there to cheer her on, but I did feel quite guilty that I was not able to be there to cheer her on. Somehow during this period of my life, I was managing to juggle family life, birding, general wildlife obsession, continuing to travel to give talks and OSME commitments. This year was busier than ever. Thankfully keeping busy seemed to help me cope better with my mental health problems, most of the time at least.

Once I got home, I was excited to discover that I had been invited to attend and give a talk at the Batumi Bird Festival in the Republic of Georgia. I did not know it at the time, but this would be my final overseas trip. After flying into Istanbul (making sure my çapulcu penguin tattoo was not on show – more on this later...), I got my next flight into Batumi. I was pleased to see that one of my Israeli friends, Jonathan Meyrav was on the flight on his way to the bird festival as well. In fact, we would be staying in the same accommodation. On arrival, once through passport control (which took an age as they seemed to take a long time examining my passport meticulously with a hand lens), we grabbed a coffee and awaited our lift up to Sakhalvasho. That was where we would be based for the festival. Our ride arrived in the form of a beat-up old Lada to take us up to Sakhalvasho near the foothills of the Lesser Caucasus to the north of Batumi. It was a bit of a scary journey. They have a very distinct driving style in Georgia! After a whistle stop tour of the area, we made it to our accommodation.

During early communications I was given a choice between staying in a hotel in Batumi or with a Georgian family in the village. This seemed a no brainer for me as living in amongst it and getting the opportunity to be educated in the local culture would add a great amount of depth to my experience. The format of the festival was to spend the days birding and wildlife watching, then congregate at the hotel in Batumi for some interesting topical talks. My highlights were a talk by Brecht Verhelst on the history of Batumi Raptor Count, Johannes Jansen spoke about the hunting concerns of the region, Jonathan Meyrav gave a great talk on long-term monitoring of soaring migratory bird migration in Israel as well as their borderless conservation work, and a fascinating talk by OSME chair, Rob Sheldon on Sociable Lapwing conservation and efforts on international flyway protection. The attendees were from an amazing range of countries including Türkiye, Belgium, Netherlands, Germany, UK, Israel, Ireland and of course Georgia. This might have been the most nervous I had been before giving a talk, it was the first time I had delivered my presentation to Türkiye people. The subject of my talk was of course 'giving my right arm for Turkish wildlife,' but also an introduction to the next stage of my project. This was my planned walk across Türkiye (from east to west). My talk seemed to be well received as indicated by the questions and discussions I engaged with afterwards.

The Batumi bottleneck sits in the northeast area of the Black Sea, the land topography funnels soaring migrating birds through the Caucasus and across the narrow section of the Black Sea. Incredibly over one million raptors are recorded from the BRC observation platforms most years.

During the time I spent at the observation posts, raptors were definitely a strong theme as one would expect! This is probably an underestimate, but I would estimate I personally observed over forty thousand Honey Buzzards. Some showed incredibly close as they flew through. It was an amazing experience seeing 'kettles' of Honey Buzzards bubbling up from the valley below in the mornings. Although the Honey Buzzards were the main event, there was an incredible supporting cast of Crested Honey Buzzard, Steppe Buzzard, Lesser Spotted Eagle, Black Kite, Montagu's Harrier, Pallid Harrier, Marsh Harrier, Eurasian Sparrowhawk, Levant's Sparrowhawk, Osprey and a *brookei* Peregrine Falcon. The passerine highlights were Green Warbler, Greater Short-toed Lark, Ehrenberg's Redstart, Roller, Hoopoe and Golden Oriole.

Unfortunately, an unpleasant undercurrent that surrounded the watch points was the widespread hunting. Whilst watching the migrating raptors from the observation platforms there would be frequent gunshots heard and sadly it was not unusual to observe a shot Honey Buzzard tumbling from the sky. This was a brutal reality of the region. Batumi Raptor Count in their NGO (non-governmental organisation) capacity were making great strides in reducing this behaviour through education and working respectfully with local community.

When I was back at my accommodation, one of the host family members walked through the room wearing a Batumi Raptor Count t-shirt and he had his rifle slung over his shoulder. He gave a wry smile as he walked through. I got the impression that some were taking things less seriously than others!

There was a Georgian wildlife filmmaker staying in the same house as me. He was very pleasant and often translated conversations with our host. He told me about the tradition of hunters using captured shrikes to lure falcons and hawks into nets for use by falconers and austringers. I dislike all forms of hunting, even when hidden behind tradition, but this method did seem to be more sustainable than blasting buzzards out of the sky.

My newfound friend asked if Jonathan and I would be interested in chatting to one of these trappers as part of the film he was making. We both agreed, I was interested to learn more about this practice. Having dabbled in falconry in the past, I did have some basic understanding. It was an education chatting to the trapper, he was incredibly open to talking to me and was actually really friendly. He was very keen to show us the very smart Goshawk that he had caught a few seasons ago. At that point in my life, I tended to try and see both sides of the argument, so perhaps I gave a little more leeway to the hunters than I would now. You cannot please everyone all the time.

We had an interesting day away from the observation platform when we visited the beautiful Chorokhi Delta. This wetland site was quite rich in Birdlife. My personal highlights were more Honey Buzzard, Black Kite, Montagu's Harrier, Pallid Harrier, Broad-billed Sandpiper, Little Crake, Corncrake, Glossy Ibis, Collared Pratincole, Rosy Starling, Lesser Grey Shrike, Citrine Wagtail and Short-toed Lark. It was fantastic to finish this daytrip with a swim in the Black Sea.

Another site we visited was Makhinjauri. Here it was amazing to see Night Herons, Nightjars, Scops Owl, and Armenian Gull flying in off the Black Sea. Eastern Black-eared Wheatear, Booted Warbler and another Nightjar was an added bonus on nearby wasteland. The festival ended with a fantastic party. Georgians know how to party! So do I as it turns out! I drank too much, danced very badly, and spoke utter nonsense. Boy did my head hurt in the morning!

The house I was hosted in may have not been what I was used to, and communication was very tricky most of the time, but I really enjoyed it and will always be grateful of the hospitality.

My trip was not quite over however as I was joining Jonathan, Jasper, Brett, Johannes, Folkert and a few other attendees from the festival, for the extension trip to Stepantsminda (also known by the soviet name of Kasbegi). Given how dangerous the roads can be in Georgia, many of us were relieved that we were traveling on the fast train to Tbilisi.

During this five-hour journey, I managed to get a little much needed sleep. The vast countryside we passed through was spectacular, this was a wonderful way to see a large portion of the country. Some of the historically significant sites that we saw included the fascinating ancient cave town at Uplistsikhe and the very much solemn sighting of the town of Gori, the birthplace of Joseph Stalin.

After arrival into Georgia's capital, Tbilisi, we picked up some food before collecting our minibus to begin the rest of the journey. Once out of the city, we joined the Georgian military road north towards the mountains. We made a few scenic stops along the road, including the spectacular Georgian-Soviet memorial near to Gudauri. We did locate some quality birds during these stops. The highlights being numbers of Raven and Asian Long-legged Buzzards, Egyptian Vulture and three displaying Lammergeier. The two vulture species were particularly special, as they were both new species for me. Once we arrived in the spectacular mountain village of Stepantsminda, we checked into our accommodation, and we had a nice evening meal and then some sleep to charge us up for a busy day of birding in the morning. The following day we checked out a couple of usually reliable sites for the Great Rosefinch but, unfortunately, we could not locate any. The highlights of what we did see was a magnificent Caucasian Ring Ouzel, an *ochuros* Black Redstart, *semirufus* Black Redstart, Caucasian Chiffchaff, Red-fronted Serin, Rock Bunting, Wryneck, Purple Heron, and Glossy Ibis. This was a nice refresher in mountain birding.

Next, we made our way up to the iconic Gergeti Trinity Church in the very necessary four-wheel drive vans. We then set off on foot carrying our camping gear, telescopes, and tripods etc, and took the path up into the high Caucasus. For me at least this was a very tough, steep climb. The effort was rewarded though, with breathtaking views and some amazing birding. We got incredible views of a pair of Lammergeier, decent views of a couple of Golden Eagles, Pallid Harrier, Montagu's Harrier and Peregrine. After the final steep climb, we were treated to views of some very tame *montana* Alpine Accentors. We arrived at our camping spot close to the Gergeti glacier. The altitude we were basing ourselves at was an impressive 10,400 ft (3,200m). The thin air was obvious to me when I was erecting my tent. I am not sure why some of us decided to put up our tents first, but it wasn't our cleverest move. We managed to miss seeing the only Güldenstädt's Redstarts of the trip. My disappointment was rapidly quashed when we got our first views of the much anticipated Caucasian Snowcock.

We spent the rest of the day and the following morning exploring some areas around the glacier. The highlights were large numbers of Caucasian Water Pipits, Caucasian Lark, *alpicola* White-winged Snow Finch, *obscura* Dunnock and more views of Caucasian Snowcock and Lammergeier. It was nice to see Hummingbird Hawkmoths frequently flying by. Camping overnight near to the glacier was not our most successful endeavour. The high altitude and sub-zero temperatures meant that most of us got very little sleep. However, it did not matter when we woke up coffee in hand to the beautiful high Caucasus sunshine.

Once we had finished birding around the glacier, we packed up all our gear, collected some delicious mountain water, and made our way off the mountains. Although this area of the Caucuses is undeniably beautiful, there was something unpleasant that just could not be ignored; it was rubbish. By this I mean there were piles of rubbish scattered around the plateau and lower tracks. I wasn't expecting to see this, and it was hugely sad.

On our way back down, we stopped to scan some slopes for grouse. This was a great decision as we had amazing views as a vocal male Caucasian Black Grouse flew over our heads before joining a few more foraging on the ridge opposite us. It was dark by the time we met with our lift back down to the village. This was good for me as I got great, albeit brief views of a very distinctive *willkonskii* Tawny Owl, a subspecies I had on my radar for this visit. Back at the accommodation, it was nice to have a warm meal and a comfortable bed after our mini expedition.

The next morning, we visited the stunning Gergeti River Valley. Here we enjoyed views of the Griffon Vulture colony as well as Caucasian Chiffchaffs, more *ochuros* Black Redstarts, Ehrenberg's

Redstart a *major* (*alpinus* group) Long-tailed Tit. There was also a trickle of Black Kites passing through the valley. The highlight for me at this site was a beautiful Camberwell Beauty butterfly. This was the first time I had seen this species since around 1992.

We returned to our accommodation for lunch before making our way back to Tiblisi. During lunch we got distracted by a pretty incredible passage of migrating raptors. Hundreds and hundreds of Black Kites made up the bulk of the migration, with smaller numbers of Greater Spotted Eagles, Lesser Spotted Eagles and Steppe Eagles.

On our way back to the city, we stopped at Ananuri to see the fortress overlooking Zhinvali Lake. Aside from a naked couple on the lakeshore, we had good views of a Georgian rarity found by Folkert, a stunning Red-rumped Swallow. A very nice end to a spectacular trip. Georgia had really left an impression on me.

Alpine Accentor in the High Caucasus

Male Pallid Harrier over the Chorokhi Delta

semirufus Black Redstart

Act Four
Unworked

During my fourth year at secondary school there was a week designated for work experience. I got the amazing opportunity to work at a local bird zoo. This was so exciting, particularly for a boy already obsessed with wildlife! Paradise Park presented itself as a conservation theme park. Mike Reynolds, an advertising copywriter, set up the bird zoo in the 1970's. Paradise Park originally known as Bird Paradise, started with a modest collection of parrots. It has grown now to accommodate over one thousand birds as well as many mammal species. The park has always had a strong conservation influence, it is the home of the World Parrot Trust, also founded by Mike.

As a visitor I was very aware of many conversation projects that the zoo participated in, such a breeding and education program for the threatened Saint Vincent Amazon Parrot. As it happened, I was assigned to the parrot section for my work experience. The week involved me assisting with the care of Hyacinth Macaws, Palm Cockatoo's, Rainbow Lorikeets, Golden Conures and many more. I got to help care for an injured Kea and African Grey Parrot. I really enjoyed my time at Paradise Park, and I thought I had found my vocation.

I started visiting the zoo every weekend on the off chance I could start working as a volunteer there to gain more experience. After pestering Jill, (the head keeper of the soft-bill section) for weeks and weeks, she finally succumbed and offered me a weekend job.

I was ecstatic! The soft-bill section looked after a very diverse range of species, basically, if it wasn't a parrot or bird of prey, it was classed as a soft bill. I worked every weekend, and my roles initially were to help prepare the food for the birds and mammals, feed them, wash up the thousand or so bowls and of course clean the enclosures. I really enjoyed this opportunity. Preparing food was a bit gruesome if I am honest, having to prepare hearts, livers, rats, and day-old cockerels. This was my first exposure to handling meat, as I was a lifelong vegetarian. I never enjoyed this aspect of the job, but I knew it was something I just had to get on with.

There were so many amazing birds that I helped to look after, but my favourites were the Northern Bald Ibis, Chough, Kori Bustard, Coscoroba Swan, Rhinoceros Hornbill, Kookaburra, Stone Curlew, Blue Crane, White-naped Crane, Sarus Crane, Victoria Crowned Pigeon, Pink Pigeon, Imperial Green Pigeon, Argus Pheasant, Bali Starling, Blond-crested Woodpecker, Livingston's Touraco, Humboldt's Penguin, Red-breasted Goose and Spreo Starling. We also looked after a few mammals, including Asian Short-clawed Otter and Goeldi's Monkey. I started to learn how to do my job well, admittedly I did make some mistakes along the way. I was very happy working at the bird park, and I felt that I had found my good place. As I continued in the job the bosses saw fit to start paying me, it was only one pound fifty a day, well you have to start somewhere!

One of the standout events that happened to me during my time at Paradise Park was not necessarily the most positive experience. I was busy pressure washing the flamingo pond, like I frequently did. It was warm sunny day, and I noticed larger numbers of Honeybees than usual around the pond. I thought nothing of it at first, until I got stung! Then I got stung repeatedly. In fact, I got stung around fifteen times! I finished the job sweltering in head-to-toe sting-proof gear. I found out later that the beekeeper had swapped the queen in the display hive the previous evening. This had of course aggravated the bees, the vibrations from the pressure washer adding another agitative stimulus.

One of my biggest highlights from working at the zoo involved the Asian Short-clawed Otters. A large family group were housed in an open enclosure near to the main entrance. This is where I cut my teeth with public speaking. At feeding time, I was often tasked with putting a microphone on and giving visitors a talk about the behaviour, ecology, and conservation of the otters. I loved this part of my job, especially when I was in amongst the charismatic group of otters. After feeding time was over, alongside another keeper, we would bring out Bubble and Squeak, our two hand-reared Asian Short-clawed Otters. As I am sure you can imagine, this was huge crowd pleaser. They were ridiculously cute and full of character. It was always entertaining when I got to clean out their enclosure. The otters were always super excited and would be running all round the space and continuously leaping onto my back, shoulders and even my head! This was such a privilege.

Once I had finished school after completing my GSCE qualifications, I decided to swerve further education and continue working at Paradise Park, with full-time hours. This was the right choice, because it really felt like I had a future in exotic animal care. Whilst working at the zoo, I got the fantastic opportunity to help fly and train some of the birds of prey with Adam, a new keeper that really did encourage my enthusiasm. I got to help with the training of young Barn Owl called Kayleigh as well as fly some incredible raptors like Bateleur's Eagle, Golden Eagle, and Lanner Falcon. The first of two eagles I found more of a challenging experience flying was Archie, the young Bald Eagle. He and his sister Grace had both been rescued in North America after they fell from a nest. Archie was quite a volatile bird, with a killer instinct. During a display flight, he landed on a Curlew in a nearby field and on another instance, he attacked one of our Humboldt Penguins (the penguin survived thankfully). Unlike the adult female Golden Eagle, Zara, who you could hold close to your face without a worry, well Archie, you could not. It was always important to keep him at arm's length and away from any ungloved limbs. I still have a scar on my finger to remind me of the day I got complacent! The second challenging aquila I had encounters with was a beautiful Tawny Eagle who was called Jason. As it turned out, Jason was a good judge of character and for reasons known only to him, he absolutely hated me. Even though I love a challenge, I didn't fly him much!

This period of my life was possibly the most content I had been and would likely ever be. I was loving my job, and my birding was just flat out exciting. I had started looking at animal husbandry courses at a local college to help further my burgeoning zookeeper career.

Nothing could stop this positive progress, could it? Well, some people say change is good and this is often the case with many people. Having learned the hard way through my life, change for me is more of a challenge. What I thrive on, and need is routine and focused direction. I did not know this at the time, but what came next would alter the direction of my life quite drastically.

As a family, we had started visiting northern Scotland during the summer holidays. We visited beautiful places like Clachtoll, Golspie, Durness and John o Groats. Exciting birds matched the amazing scenery, like Red Grouse, Hen Harriers and Osprey's. I was always super hyped during these holidays as I never really knew what I would see. What I didn't anticipate is what came next. My family were relocating to northern Scotland. I was quite upset that I would not get to continue my work at Paradise Park, but, naively, I was quite excited about what lay ahead of me.

Whilst living in Scotland I attended both Elmwood Agricultural in Cupar and the Scottish Agricultural College at Auchincruive, Where I studied various levels of conservation management

88

courses. This was quite a different to what I had done previously, but it did seem my best option at the time. I lived in Perthshire for a time, and I began to spend a lot of time at a local nature reserve called Loch of Lowes.

This Scottish Wildlife Trust (SWT) nature reserve was famous for its regular breeding pair of Ospreys. I volunteered there for a while and was subsequently employed on a short contract for Osprey security, it was for a very meagre wage, but it was an incredible opportunity. The collection of most wild bird eggs was outlawed in Britain in 1954 with the Protection of Birds Act (1954) and by the inception of the Wildlife and Countryside Act in 1981, it became illegal to own or control the eggs of any wild birds. The problem with laws, is they are frequently ignored. Egg collecting is, unfortunately no different and in some cases, it can be quite lucrative. Egg collectors are usually very organised and truly knowledgeable about bird ecology. If they could be trusted, some of these people could be a real asset to bird conservation. Egg thieves are never content with taking just one egg from a nest, they take the whole clutch. Considering they usually target rare breeding birds, the impact their obsession has on these declining species can be disastrous. One of the species that was a prime target for egg thief's, was the exquisite Osprey.

The Osprey is without any shadow of a doubt, the most impressive raptor species found in the northern hemisphere. The osprey is a highly successful species on a global scale, it has quite a cosmopolitan distribution. They breed across Eurasia, Australasia and Northern and Central America. Ospreys have unfortunately had a more troublesome history in Britain. The Western Osprey became extinct as a breeding species in the UK by 1916 due to relentless persecution. Thanks to conservation efforts, these striking white and brown diurnal raptors returned as a breeding species to Scotland in 1954. Since then, the Scottish population has increased to a stable 400-500 pairs. At the time of writing the

Osprey has breeding pairs away from the core population in the Highlands scattered throughout Southern Scotland, England and Wales. There is also breeding pairs in the Rutland area as the result of a successful, yet probably unnecessary reintroduction project.

The Osprey is a very distinctive medium to large bird of prey that is a fish specialist with some specific evolutionary adaptations. These include the outer front toe that can swivelled backwards to enable a better grip on its fish prey, the nictitating membrane that protect their eyes when they dive into water, and the thick oily feathers that allow them to dry out quickly and prevent waterlogging. They are incredible birds.

Loch of Lowes was a great mix of upland oak woodland and freshwater lochs. These woodlands were full of birdsong in the spring and summer months. Chiffchaff, Willow Warbler, Wood Warbler, Sedge Warbler, Treecreeper, Pied Flycatcher and Redstart were all easily seen. Many of the birds were species that I had not seen many times before.

My duties on the reserve in my Osprey security capacity was to manage the amazing team of volunteers to make sure the Osprey's were guarded during daylight hours and I covered the night and morning shift. It was usually a long night, but the morning could often be rewarding with fantastic views of Roe Deer and Otters. I once had a male Pied Flycatcher hovering inches from my nose during a particularly sunny early morning, just one of many incredible experiences during my time on the nature reserve.

Egg thieves are usually obsessive types, but there were also some criminals that would steal to order. These people were clearly driven by greed or obsession, so there was a clear potential threat to our safety whilst we were preventing the osprey eggs being stolen. For that reason, we would conduct our patrols around the perimeter of the reserve armed with some fairly fierce home-made baseball bats. That was, at least, until we got some friendly advice from an off-duty police officer. We had a good relationship with the local police force, and we wanted it to stay that way! The nightshift was always a bit of a challenge, dark hours that brought a healthy bucket of fear.

It turns out that Sedge Warblers sing all night. Not intermittently, but constantly, they never ever stop! That can send an osprey protector over the edge! When I first started the night watch I just had to rely on my ears to identify any potential threats to the osprey nest. I loved the simplicity and purity of that but understood the need for some technology.

The first bit of kit that was built and installed by a local electrician and one of our volunteers, was a microphone. The microphone itself was positioned at the base of the tree that held the osprey nest and the speaker box was positioned near to my watch point. This gave us much better security as we knew we would clearly hear if anyone was attempting to access the nest. Due to the length of cable needed, the speaker also produced a strong signal of the BBC World Service!

Not ideal, but the entertainment did help me through the dark hours. Later, an infrared closed-circuit camera was installed, this was the ultimate bit of technology without a doubt, but staring at a screen for hours and hours was soul destroying. Although, we were able to confirm that there were Pine Marten's present on the reserve, when we saw two of them climbing the osprey tree! Thankfully, they were unable to get past all the razor wire.

The Pine Marten is classified in the *mustalidae* (mustelids) family which also includes Badgers, Otters, Stoats and Wolverines. At around 52cm (21 in) in length it is a sizeable mammal, and this coupled with its chocolate-brown coat, bushy tail and large creamy-yellow throat patch make it unmistakable. They are woodland specialist omnivores, seldom found outside of this habitat. Globally this species is found across most of Europe and Asia Minor as well as parts of Iraq, Iran and Syria. The Pine Marten also has a restricted population in Ireland. Within a British context the marten was formally widespread throughout, unfortunately because of hunting and woodland clearances they declined significantly, and the core population retracted to the Scottish Highlands. There is good news thankfully, as due to protection and habitat conservation work, the Pine Marten can now be found over much of Scotland as well as relict populations increasing in Wales, Shropshire, Northumberland, Yorkshire and Cumbria.

I kept myself going through the night by smoking Golden Virginia or Drum tobacco and drinking copious amounts of instant coffee. All disgusting and ill-advised habits, but they definitely helped at the time. Working night consistently for days and weeks, took a bit of a toll on my energy levels and my sanity. The strangest things I experienced happened just as it was getting light one morning. I noticed two reasonably sized animals swimming across the loch, after closer inspection I was certain they were a pair of rhinoceroses! Of course, they weren't rhinos, that would be ridiculous. They were Roe Deer; my tired brain was just struggling to process what my eyes were seeing! It was always an anxious wait for daylight, particularly in the pre-technology days. Seeing one of our Osprey's sat tightly on their nest, continuing to incubate their eggs was not only hugely satisfying, but also a great relief.

I felt like I had a lot of responsibility on my seventeen-year young shoulders. Although egg thieves and their activities were constantly on my mind, I only had one occasion when I was confronted my some. It was around two-thirty in the morning, and I was at my station listening out for disturbances as usual. I heard footsteps that seemed to come out of a restricted access area of woodland, then directly towards my position. I assumed it was Dave or some other member of the team. It was not, I was met by two men who I had never seen before.

One of them seemed quite tall and he positioned himself directly in the way of my only exit, and the shorter, stockier man stood over my shoulder. If they were trying to intimidate me, they had succeeded. They asked me a lot of probing questions about what I was doing, questions about osprey security and related things. It was clear to me that these characters were egg thieves, I mean, who just drops into a nature reserve at the early hours of the morning just because they were passing through? I knew that it would be risky calling for back up, as by the time support arrived, I could be at the receiving end of a physical pummelling! I answered their questions, the best I could without divulging sensitive information. Eventually they left and once they were far enough away, I called up on the radio and reported the incident.

The police were alerted, and they caught up the two men as they walked back to their car that was parked around three miles away. Their car was searched and found to have no contents that could be used for egg thievery. It is likely they were on a reconnaissance mission; you wouldn't load up your vehicle with incriminating evidence until you actually needed it after all. I was told that the police held these two known egg thieves overnight, but they left without charge the following morning. Hopefully that experience put the frights up them enough to dissuade them from another visit.

Thankfully, the rest of the incubation period continued without any more excitement and the osprey pair hatched two healthy chicks. Relief, pride, gratitude, and elation were the main mix of emotions I was experiencing at the time.

After my contract ended on the reserve I stayed on for the rest of the summer in a voluntary capacity. I would spend a lot of time chatting to visitors, trying to recruit new members to the Scottish Wildlife Trust, something I seemed quite good at. I also enjoyed engaging with other volunteers, we had some very interesting people helping out on the nature reserve. One of the most enjoyable aspects of volunteering is that I got the opportunity to conduct the monthly wetland birds survey (WeBS) run by the Wildfowl and Wetlands Trust (WWT). The survey site I covered followed a route linking Mill Dam, Rotmell Loch and Dowally Loch. This area always felt really remote, and I always enjoyed the anticipation. I would often see Osprey's hunting over the small lochs as well as regular sightings of Peregrine Falcon and Merlin. The supporting cast of Great Spotted Woodpeckers, Redstart's, Stonechats, Whinchats and Twite made for an exciting walk.

Following my first season at Loch of Lowes, I went on to work as a long-term volunteer for the National Trust for Scotland (NTS) on their A9 properties.

The nature reserves we looked after were the Hermitage, Killiecrankie and the Linn of Tummel. I stayed in one of the 'little houses' in Dunkeld during my stint. Ben, my boss was hugely enthusiastic about the reserves and his enthusiasm was infectious. The job involved general estate maintenance, including, building paths and steps, wildlife surveys, including intriguing species like Bird's-nest Orchids, and my favourite, leading guided walks and working with school groups. These reserves were not only rich in wildlife, but they were steeped in human history, the Jacobite rebellion at Killiecrankie being the most significant. I enjoyed this mixture of wildlife and human history. Leading guided walks for the general public and working with school groups was part of my responsibilities that I really enjoyed. I think some of my experience from working at Paradise Park really helped me with this. I enjoyed my three months volunteering with the National Trust for Scotland, and I felt like Ben had taught me a lot more about practical wildlife conservation than I had learnt at college, nothing beats learning in real world context.

During my time in Dunkeld, I also got myself involved in my first real relationship, she was a trainee dentist from Dundee, and I really liked her. Unfortunately, it didn't last that long due to me being too young and too stupid to know what I was doing!

For the following season I had accepted a job offer to become one of the Seasonal Wardens at Loch of Lowes. I was experiencing imposter syndrome, but it just felt good working on the reserve again. The summer went well, with the Osprey's breeding successfully again.

This familiar chorus line by The Specials could describe the next period of my life! During my time working at Loch of Lowes, I had met a girl, Karen, who was working at one of the local hotels. We ended up getting into a committed relationship quite quickly, too quickly some may say! I had a habit of jumping into things feet first without thinking things through! After my contract ended with the Scottish Wildlife Trust we lived in a bedsit in Dunkeld for a while. I spent a lot of time in the local pubs, especially when a friend started working as a bartender and plied me with unlimited pints of Guinness! I do not remember a lot about those days, but it was certainly the first time my mental health problems really concerned me during early adulthood.

We moved to Glencarse, which sits between Perth and Dundee, and we lived in a farm flat. We got on well with our neighbour and I joined him quite a few times as a labourer, helping him clear out houses that had been damaged by the infamous floods in 1993. It was a tough job, dealing with waterlogged house contents and the stink and filth that went side by side with that. I enjoyed having a more purpose for a while.

Whilst living in Glencarse Karen and I succumbed to the social norms and got married at Perth registry office. I think my mother could see that our relationship was not a stable one when she asked me if I was sure, I wanted to go ahead with the wedding, as she drove me to the registry office. Of course, I did have big concerns and massive doubts, but I didn't want to let anyone down and I also felt that at the age of 21, this was my last opportunity not to be left on my own for the rest of my life. My mind was quite broken already. We got married and had a big ole party!

After I finished my contract at Loch of Lowes, Karen and I moved to Galashiels in the Scottish Borders. This was the town Karen was originally from. Karen fell pregnant with our first child around this time. This was something we were very excited about. However, at the seven months check up at the doctor's surgery, they told us something was wrong, there was no heartbeat. In hospital, they told us our baby had died. This was devastating to both of us. Karen still had to go through the process of labour, to give birth to our baby. I really cannot imagine how terrible an experience this must have been for her. This might sound morbid to most, but we spent the following day with our perfectly formed, but freezing cold dead baby, Dylan. This was important, but at the same something that I would not wish on my worst enemy.

The funeral some days later, was one of the hardest things I have ever had to attend. Part of me died the day Dylan died and I have never been able to deal with this huge loss.

We stayed with Karen's mum and stepdad for a little while, before moving to Rutherford Mains. Rutherford Mains sits along the river Tweed, west of Kelso. There were logistical problems living out there because there was not a very regular bus service and neither of us could drive. I would frequently have to walk the seven miles or so into Kelso, fill up my big rucksack with heavy shopping and then walk back. I was a lot fitter in those days! Rutherford Mains was a nice quiet place to live, surrounded by nice rural landscapes. There was a bird rich walk along the old disused railway line and the nearby river Tweed frequently attracted Whooper Swans and

Goosander. The grounds of Floors Castle in Kelso were particularly special, particularly as they were a reliable site for Nuthatch and Marsh Tit, both very scarce breeding birds in Scotland at the time.

After moving to a flat in Galashiels for a brief time, we hit the housing and birding jackpot when we got the opportunity to move to the coastal village of Coldingham. Exciting times ahead! Coldingham is a small village on the east coast of the Scottish Borders. The village is positioned close to the prominent headland of St Abb's head. This was a dream location for me and my first experience of east coast birding. I knew some of the birding history of the headland, told to me by Tim Drew, who had previously worked on the reserve as a seasonal warden. In fact, he found and identified Britain's third ever record of Marmora's Warbler on the headland a few years prior. This was the rarest bird to be found at St Abb's. At the time St Abb's Head was co-managed by the National Trust for Scotland and the Scottish Wildlife Trust.

The SWT seemed keen to have a presence on the reserve, so they invited me to spend time there in a voluntary capacity. This was fine with me, as I got to spend more time on the reserve. Not long after moving into our new home in Coldingham, I went for a little explore of the nearby Coldingham Bay. This was a small, secluded beach, lined with brightly coloured beach huts. The first bird I encountered here, was a smart winter plumaged Slavonian Grebe. This was a nice start. The Slavonian Grebe, also known as the Horned Grebe, can be found on breeding territories in cool temperate and subarctic regions of North America (including Canada), Iceland, the Faroe Islands, Scandinavia, Russia and northernmost China. There is also a small breeding population in northern Scotland. During winter, the species is found in coastal waters a little further south of their breeding range. I would spend a lot of time on the headland, getting increasingly obsessed with finding my own rare birds. This was a big red flag, indicating that my mental health issues may be a little more serious than I thought. That aside, I did have an amazing time searching the headland every day and meeting some like-minded people.

Our marriage had not really recovered very well from the death of our first son, Dylan. When Karen was pregnant with our second child, I hoped this would help to repair the damage. Our baby was born healthy at the Borders General Hospital and we named him Lachlan. I was too young and naive to do a decent job at being a good father, though I did try. I used to take Lachlan with me when I went shopping and even when I went birding at St Abb's Head. I was not coping well with my responsibilities at home, and I was spending more and more time birding along the coast. St Abb's had become my solace, perhaps because I may have been trying to escape home life that was becoming more and more challenging. At this point, I knew my marriage was struggling and the thought of spending the rest of my life with Karen, did not fill me with joy. Rightly or wrongly, I was just going to have to style it out for the sake of Lachlan. I had enjoyed my time birding at St Abb's, but sadly, like all good things, they rarely last forever.

The person that we rented our home from had a change in circumstances, so she was unable to accommodate our tenancy anymore. This was incredibly sad news, as I had really found my place in the world there. Things were still not great with my marriage and what came next would either make it or break it (spoiler alert, it broke it...). We had to move out quickly. I think the writing on the wall was already there and glowing in neon lights at this stage, although I was oblivious to it as usual. Karen wanted to go and stay with her Mum in Galashiels until we found a suitable property. I did not want to return there, so I decided to go back to Glen Quaich and stay with my parents for a while. I thought, a little break would do our relationship good. It is possible that subconsciously I was thinking the opposite.

Being back in Perthshire was nice for a while, though I was missing the buzz of east coast birding. I thought things were progressing positively with my marriage as we got on well during our frequent telephone conservations. I remember being very happy when I received a valentine's card from Karen through the post. This was short-lived as a day or so later she told me she didn't love me anymore and wanted to separate permanently. I should have seen this coming, and I should have been happy, but I didn't, and I wasn't. I was devastated and heartbroken, not only was my marriage destroyed, but I would miss so much of my son growing up. I lost a part of myself right there and my rejection anxiety had a lifetime supply of fuel.

When I was at Bishop Burton College in Yorkshire, studying for a BSc (Hons) in Ornithology, a part time job at the library there was advertised, it definitely piqued my interest. I applied for the position and was invited in for an interview. This was new ground for me as I'd never actually had a job interview before. All my previous employments I'd got through pestering or volunteering first! This interview went very well, and I didn't have to wait long before I was offered the job. Working in the library really suited me, it was generally a quiet and peaceful environment, allowing me to get on with the tasks of restocking the bookshelves and keeping the rooms tidy.

I got myself involved in a few relationships during this time, none of which lasted particularly long. That was until I met Kath! After I settled into my new digs in Walkington, I spent a lot of time with my college friends who lived nearby in a house share. During my frequent visits I got to meet Kathleen, an equine science student that lived in the house with my friends. Kathleen was quite shy and was very pretty, although she never saw that herself. There was something interesting about her, I liked her, and I thought she liked me too. At the end of my first week in Walkington I went into Beverley with Kathleen, her friend Linda and my mate Dan.

We were out to celebrate Linda's birthday. It was a great night and with the alcohol flowing and confidence primed, Kathleen and I embarked on a shiny new relationship, she had no idea what adventures awaited her! Joking aside, because my previous two long-term relationships had ended so badly, and I had consequently been left emotionally hurt, I knew that I had to take this new relationship steadily.

My plan was to have fun and not get too emotionally invested. Wasn't it John Lennon that said 'life happens whilst you are busy making plans? If it was, he was not wrong! Within a few weeks I had moved out of my digs and moved in with Kath, oh, and we had gotten engaged too. In hindsight it would seem that I have little control over my emotions and impulses, and I am proficient at ignoring my inner monologue. Of course, it is not all on me, Kath had clearly succumbed to my rugged good looks and wily charms! On a more serious note, we never did get married, but we are still happily and defiantly living in sin some twenty-four plus years later, despite the problems of me.

During late spring I had managed to get myself a job working for the Yorkshire Wildlife Trust at Spurn Point. Not my dream job as such, but certainly my dream location at the time. Kath also joined me at the observatory, and she managed to secure some summer work at the Riverside Hotel in Kilnsea. My job was basic, collecting admission fees from people wanting to drive to the point. As there were a lot of ground nesting birds on the reserve, there were no dogs allowed, so I had to enforce that rule as well. Not the most glamorous job, but the benefit was getting plenty of time on the reserve to see interesting birds. Late spring and early summer seemed quite a productive time at Spurn, certainly in the year 2000 it was.

During the first month or so of working there I managed to see some good scarcities and drift migrants. These included Red-backed Shrike, Golden Oriole, Wryneck, Honey Buzzard and the declining Turtle Dove. This was a genuinely nice start to my time staying at Spurn. My boss at the time was Barry Spence, he was a birder and bird ringer with a big passion for the peninsula where he had been the warden for decades. It is fair to say that Barry did not suffer fools gladly and he certainly appeared to be very gruff on the outside at least. However, my experience of Barry was that he was fair, kind and he had a very dry sense of humour. Whenever a rare bird was found on the reserve, he always allowed me to leave my post at the Warren to see it. During the week when there were less visitors and conditions looked favourable, he gave me all clear to walk up to the peninsula to see if there were any interesting birds to be found. This was of course under the understanding that I did not let any cars through for free!

It wasn't all about birds though, there was a pond not far from the Warren called Clubley's scrape, this was a very good place to see dragonflies and damselflies. Barry introduced me to the excitement of finding and identifying species from this group. Dragonflies are undoubtedly a birders gateway drug to a broader wildlife interest, a dangerous thing for my personality type!

The reserve supported a range of common species which included Azure Damselfly, Common Blue Damselfly, Blue-tailed Damselfly, Emerald Damselfly, Large Red Damselfly, Emperor Dragonfly, Migrant Hawker, Four-spotted Chaser, Black-tailed Skimmer, Common Darter, and Ruddy Darter. The scarce migrant, Red-veined Darter was also frequent, and I remember a handful of sightings of the scarce (at the time) Broad-bodied Chaser. I spent many quieter bird days looking for *odonata*! Barry also ran a moth trap at the Warren, this was a light trap that attracted moths live. Once identified the moths could then be carefully released back into suitable habitat. I do not think I was quite ready for the steep learning curve of moth identification, but Barry often showed me some of the more interesting species that he'd caught. These included Lime Hawk Moth, Convolvulus Hawk Moth and the locally scarce Birdswing Moth.

There were definitely some spring and summer birding highlights that are fixed in my memory banks. The thing with Spurn was that it would sometimes throw up some unexpected surprises. One Sunday, during late afternoon after I'd finished work, I was walking down the canal bank to have another look for the White-rumped Sandpiper that had been found earlier in the day. Adam Hutt called me up on the radio to let me know that there was an exceptional passage of terns past the sea watching hide. After watching a Roseate Tern flying onto the Humber, I quickly made my way to the sea watching hide. I was so glad I did too, as almost as soon as I arrived, Adam had locked onto an interesting swift flying near to Beacon Ponds and making its way towards us. It was a small brown swift with a paler chin, with quite a chunky body and a short tail and I had absolutely no clue to its identity. Thankfully, there were wiser birders amongst us, Adam, Nick Bell and a few others discussed the identification and concluded that we were watching a Chimney Swift.

Of course, this made sense once they had confirmed the identification! The Chimney Swift breeds in eastern North America and migrates to the Amazon basin regions of Chile and Brazil. This was the first Chimney Swift recorded in Yorkshire and only the twelfth British record. What a Chimney Swift was doing on the east coast of Yorkshire in late summer we will always be uncertain about, but it is fair to suggest that it arrived in Europe the previous autumn and lingered somewhere before acting on its urge to migrate. Whatever the circumstances it was one of the most fascinating and exciting birding experiences I'd had!

Through Richard Baines from Flamborough, I soon began a new job as a bird surveyor. This was at the start of the wind power revolution, so it will come as no surprise that all the sites I worked on were proposed windfarm developments. All the projects I worked on with this company were on the mountainous areas of Scotland. It was great to be back in the north. The survey's that I was tasked to conduct involved raptors and wading birds. For the wading birds we used an upland wader transect methodology standardised by Andrew Brown and Kevin Shepherd. This involved covering the survey site within a hundred metres of the point of travel, all wader species seen or heard would be recorded onto a map. For the raptors, we used a methodology called vantage point survey. This involved sitting on the top of a hill for usually three or six hours and recording the flight path of any birds of prey observed. It was great being up in the high hills again and more so that I was able to contribute to our income again.

As you would expect in the harsher habitat in the Scottish Highlands, the species encountered were not hugely diverse, but there were definitely some exciting creatures seen. My personal highlights were Golden Eagle, Osprey, Hen Harrier, Red Kite, Goshawk, Dunlin, Golden Plover, Curlew, Dipper, and Common Sandpiper.

I had struggled with my education. Mostly due a flare up of my bipolar symptoms (although I wasn't aware of this at the time}. I knew my behaviours were becoming more outlandish and I was attempting to seek escape through alcohol. This wasn't the smart choice, and it eventually came to a head when I failed my penultimate year of my degree course. Kath had graduated and found a job in Coventry, so I decided that taking a break from education and moving to the midlands with her was my most sensible option.

Apart from a brief residence in Dundee, this was the first time I'd lived in in a city. For me it was quite a big culture shock, and I did struggle to deal with it at times. Kath had long since started her new job, whilst I struggled to find employment. Thankfully, there was a decent bus service, and I could escape to the countryside to get my fix of wildlife. I spent most of my days exploring Brandon Marsh, a local nature reserve that was cared for by Warwickshire Wildlife Trust. This was a great little reserve, comprising of pools, broadleaf woodland, and some grassland meadows. Birdlife was quite varied due to the range of habitat; the most notable species was Cetti's Warbler. These were present in quite high densities; this is the only site I am aware of where seeing this notoriously elusive species was relatively easy. Their song is also incredibly explosive and always exciting to hear. As with most natural areas, it was not just about the birds. Brandon Marsh has a rich biodiversity.

One of the more prominent and interesting species groups encountered were dragonflies and damselflies. On the reserve I was pleased to see familiar species such as Blue-tailed Damselfly, Common Blue Damselfly, Azure Damselfly, Large Red Damselfly, Southern Hawker, Emperor Dragonfly, Common Darter, Ruddy Darter, Red-veined Darter, and Black-tailed Skimmer. Equally I was excited to discover some new to me species such as Red-eyed Damselfly and Brown Hawker. One other noteworthy and regular wildlife encounter was observing Grass Snakes swimming in the pools. This was always fascinating to see.

I did manage to continue with the ecological consultancy work, when I was needed and I also did a little casual work with a new birder friend, Mike. It was mostly park maintenance or conservation management type work. I really enjoyed this, and I was super grateful for that opportunity.

The news that Kath was carrying our first child together was incredible, in fact we were ecstatic. With this change in our circumstances, we had to make some tricky decisions. Ideally, I would have preferred a move back to Yorkshire or Cornwall for my own obvious reasons, but it was very clear that Kath needed to be close to her Mum for this life changing period in our lives. So, it was decided, we started to get our ducks in a row and began planning the next chapter in our life that started with a big move to Cumbria. Daunting, but certainly exciting times ahead.

Prior to our move North, I had secured employment with a small ecology consultancy firm on the Solway coast. It was an eccentric set up and my role was quite a mix of things. Firstly, I was tasked with answering the phone and helping with project management. I also helped with some of the ongoing avian surveys, mostly and delightfully on landfill sites!

Cumbria was, at that time, home to one of England's only known (or only publicised at least) Golden Eagles. There had been a pair there for many years, though at this stage, the female had vanished, leaving only the male.

During our visit to Haweswater, it was a brilliant sunny summers day. We enjoyed the walk that provided stunning scenery on our way to the Royal Society for the Protection of Birds (RSPB) viewpoint. We were soon enjoying decent views of the resident Golden Eagle. Whilst I was buzzing from the experience, I am pretty sure that a fairly heavily pregnant Kathleen was questioning her life choices. In hindsight I should have been a lot more considerate to Kath's needs and a lot less focused on my blinkered obsession with birds. Having learned nothing from this experience, next we were walking up to the Dodd Wood Osprey viewpoint to get ridiculously distant views of what were then England's only natural breeding pair of Osprey's at the time. We later discovered that much closer views could be achieved from a layby on the opposite side of Bassenthwaite Lake. With all this apparent craziness behind me, for the time being at least, there was something very significant that was about to happen in our lives.

It was mid-September and Kathleen had started having contractions. Things rapidly got real. Thankfully, we were fairly prepared, and we soon arrived at the maternity ward. This was the first instant that I realised Kathleen was made of incredibly tough stuff (in retrospect the first instant should have been the fact that she stayed with me despite my obvious short comings). I tried to support Kath the best I could whilst she bravely powered on through labour. Many hours later all her relentless efforts paid out in bucket loads, with the birth of our first daughter, Shannon. Shannon was a beautiful little baby, with a full, thick head of ginger hair. More importantly both baby and mother were in good health. I am still astounded by Kath's strength in going through childbirth, I can only guess at how terrifying it must be for a young mother, knowing what she is going to have to cope with, let alone actually physically going through it. At this point in time, we were ecstatic that our family had grown by one. Although I knew that the birth of Shannon would change our life's forever, I had no idea how important our cute little girl would be to the richness of our lives in the many years to come. After a decent spell of paternity leave, I was back at work.

The following spring work life was getting a bit of a struggle for me, and this was made worse by issues I had with my boss. Things got very serious an in the end I had no choice but to resign from the job. I should've have thought about the financial implications before making the decision, but this was most definitely an emotionally charged reaction. Family life was all positive as far as I was aware. Shannon was growing fast and turning into a bright, characterful, and creative individual. In retrospect I should have been spending more time at home supporting Kath and less time watching birds.

After resigning from my job on the Solway, I began doing some freelance avian ecology work for a renewable energy development company based in North Wales and central Scotland. This meant spending a lot of time away from home, not an ideal situation, but at least the money was decent. This change of employment was definitely a marker for the next intriguing chapter of my life. It's a new day and a new dawn and all that.

I started my new employment and there was some definite familiarity with this job, I was back doing adapted Brown and Shepherd wader surveys as well as vantage point raptor surveys.

106

When I met the team, I was working with, I was surprised and happy to see that I knew one of the surveyors, although I knew his brother better from my Perthshire days, he had accompanied for my first trip to Foula, back when I was working for the Scottish Wildlife Trust. He was a fantastic quirky character, very keen rare bird finding obsessive and very sharp. I was looking forward to working and birding with Tim and the team.

The first few sites I was tasked with surveying in the southern uplands, the Scottish Borders, and West Lothian. Most of these sites were not that biodiverse, mainly because much of the habitat had been degraded by overgrazing. Despite these areas not being particularly exciting, they provided a good opportunity for me to sharpen my skillset after quite a long break from conducting these specific ecological surveys. There were the usual expected upland breeding birds on most of our survey sites, like Whinchat, Dipper, Grey Wagtail and Redstart's, but both raptors and waders tended to be quite sparse. Of course, these observations were ideal for developers trying to get a windfarm project approved, but it was unfortunately a sad indictment on the state of nature in many of these upland habitats. After continuing working on these three sites for some time, the company must have been happy with my reliability and standard of work as they asked me to join the team as a full-time salaried employee. After weighing up my options, I took the opportunity and joined the team. I knew there would be exciting times ahead. My normal life was also continuing on a similar vein.

Family life was going strong and changing somewhat. Kathleen was pregnant with our second child together and Shannon was growing up fast and continuing to develop into the quirky and unique character that we all know and love today. I continued working for the development company based out of Edinburgh and our list of sites was getting more interesting. We had sites in Perthshire, Sutherland, Ayrshire, the Scottish Borders, Dumfries and

Galloway, Stirlingshire, Sutherland and Argyle and Bute. These sites were quite varied, but some were surprisingly good for seeing some exciting birds such as, Golden Eagles, Hen Harriers, Osprey's, Red Kites, Honey Buzzard, Merlin and even Black Grouse. Staying away from home so much was quite difficult at times, but I did enjoy the work, at least at first. I was able to take time off when our second beautiful baby, Erin was born.

As time passed, the company went through some changes and the stress and pressure on me started to build. I was beginning to feel out of my depth in the job. Looking back now, a big sign that something was not right in my world, was when I got shingles. Shingles often rears its ugly head on people suffering with stress. I thought nothing of it at the time and once recovered I returned to work.

As the week's passed, I could not ignore the fact that something was wrong with me. I eventually went to my doctor, to check it was not serious. The symptoms I had were tiredness and being physically sick in the mornings before work. After asking me some questions the doctor gave me the diagnosis of clinical depression. I was promptly signed off work. This was not what I was expecting. Little did I realise that this would be the beginning of an incredibly challenging part of my life. I was signed off work consistently week after week and sadly, in the end I had no choice but to resign. What I had not anticipated was that my health would deteriorate to such an extent, that I would still be unable to function in the workforce over twelve years later!

I was not working because I didn't want to, I wasn't working because I was too ill to. This troubled me from the start, and it troubles me now. I felt like I had failed as a human being, I mean, I couldn't even provide for my children. This feeling of failure would be further strengthened by some peoples obvious and misguided opinions, that they believed that I was lazy and that I should get a job. If only it was that simple.

Act Five
Tattoomanic

As may you have already picked up on, my first wildlife trip to Türkiye had a big impact on me. When I returned from that trip, I spoke to my friend Charlie Moores, to tell him about the exciting wildlife I had observed, beautiful scenery I'd seen and amazing people I'd met. He was happy that I'd had such a good holiday, but then informed me of an ecological and social disaster that was unfolding in the country. This would have a devastating impact on wildlife and rural communities at both a local and global level. I was devastated to learn that the Turkish government had sold off all the country's waterways to private corporations. There were over 2,000 dams being built, and over 1,730 hydro-electric schemes planned. The impact this would cause would be disastrous. Not only would the habitats of one of the most biodiverse countries in the Western Palearctic be damaged beyond repair, but many small communities were likely to be displaced, thus destroying these traditional and important, localised cultures.

To put things into context, Türkiye was at the time, home to, 30% of the global population of the endangered (formally critically endangered) Northern Bald Ibis and more than 90% of the global population of the Cinereous Bunting. Additionally, the country held 25% of the European breeding population of the endangered White-headed Duck, more than 10% of the global population of the endangered Egyptian Vulture, more than 70% of the global population of the near-endemic and near threatened Krüper's Nuthatch and more than 30% of the global population of Eurasian Rollers. Türkiye also holds five endemic mammals (mountains there are reported still to hold the Anatolian or Asia Minor Leopard), 52 endemic freshwater fish, 13 endemic reptiles and over 30 endemic plants. Hydroelectric power is not in reality the environmentally friendly solution to renewable energy production it is frequently marketed as.

The displacement of endemic communities that have been caring for the local biodiversity for years, is usually not even a considered impact. Also, when a valley is flooded to create a reservoir, the vegetation rots down, potentially releasing massive amounts of carbon (that would otherwise be locked away) into the atmosphere. Further problems can occur when the movement of silt is impacted and significant reduction in water levels can hugely degrade on the ecology of the riparian habitat and surrounding areas. In the context of Türkiye, beside the local land, the biodiversity of countries further downstream (such as Syria and Iraq) would be under severe threat.

Armed with this devastating information, I knew that I needed to help in some way. Having just visited Türkiye and still been unaware of this ongoing ecological disaster, I knew that it was fair to assume that few other people would be aware of the situation. I knew that my main job had to be raising awareness. Secondary to this, but almost as important was raising funds to help a Turkish wildlife conservation charity with their vital work.

After a bit of research, I chose the Birdlife International partner in Türkiye, Doğa Derneği. The name of this organisation translates as 'nature society.' I really liked how passionate this charity was, how active they were and most importantly, how they had a real focus on involving local communities with their conservation projects. I'm not classically creative, meaning I have no traditional

110

talent or skill. However, when my mood is elevated, I tend to have the ability to think more creatively than usual.

Whilst going for a walk along one of the local country lanes, my brain was bombarded with lots of potential ideas, some more extreme than others! I settled on a unique idea that I named 'giving my right arm for Turkish wildlife.' The plan was to get my right arm tattooed with as many iconic Turkish birds as possible. For context, I had no previous experience of tattoos, I may have fantasised about getting one or two before but felt I didn't have the physique to carry it off!

When my mood is up all rationality disappears and it tends to be an all or nothing approach. True to form, I did not discuss this project with anyone, until I had publicly announced it and was fully committed. I just had to find a good tattoo artist. It is interesting how sometimes things just fall into place. Having started some research on local tattoo studios, I realised that stepping through the door could be the hardest part of this project. I mean, I did not look like the sort of person I imagined would get tattooed. Thankfully, none of this overthinking would be of any relevance overall.

I was super organised with this new obsession, and I had put out a lot of press releases, if I was going to do this, I wanted to maximise the impact it could have. I was pleased when the local BBC television news team contacted me with an interest in interviewing me. We arranged a suitable time, and they came around to my home. The journalist enquired as to whether I had a tattoo artist in mind. At this stage I had not. He told me of a new studio that had opened near to his office and asked if I would be willing to be filmed chatting to the artists. This was a great idea, and the following day I was introduced to Richard Batey and Rob Richardson. Rob had some fantastic finch tattoos on one of his arms that had been inked by Richard. Once I had chatted with Richard about my plans, he was super hyped and seemed completely on board. He was a bit of an activist and even offered to donate twenty pounds to my cause for every hour he tattooed me.

I knew he had the skills, and he definitely had the passion, so I booked in for a consultation. At the same time, I was also trying to decide which species of Turkish birds I would have tattooed into my skin. My only strict rule was that they had to be birds I had seen. I needed a good memory attached to them. I curated a shortlist of forty Turkish birds, then I ran a poll on my website to enable my readers to make the final decision. In the end we decided to include twenty-four species. These were White-throated Robin, Radde's Accentor, Pied Kingfisher, Smyrna Kingfisher, Wallcreeper, Masked Shrike, Desert Finch, Asian Crimson-winged Finch, Northern Bald Ibis, Pallid Scops Owl, Crag Martin, Little Swift, Krüper's Nuthatch, Black Francolin, Caspian Snowcock, Rüppell's Warbler, Menetries's Warbler, Red-fronted Serin, Eastern Rock Nuthatch, Cinereous Bunting, Dead sea Sparrow, Roller and White-winged Snowfinch. I was going to need a bigger arm!

Before my consultation with Richard, I had already decided that I would be offering up both my arms to the project. Once I chatted with Richard, we agreed on what birds would be tattooed where, I paid my deposit and booked my first session. At this point in the process my mood was persistently high, my depressive symptoms seemed to have disappeared, I was feeling exceptionally good. Because of my fundraising project, I was staying up late on my computer, using various social network platforms to promote what I was doing. I seemed to not require as much sleep. I was oblivious to all this at the time, all that mattered was 'giving my right arm.' With hindsight these were clear symptoms that there was something seriously wrong with my behaviour. It would be sometime before this would be accurately diagnosed.

My first tattoo session soon arrived, and I was incredibly nervous, I knew it would be uncomfortable, but I really wasn't sure what to expect. A tattoo machine on average punctures the upper layer of skin between fifty and three thousand times a minute. I probably shouldn't have done a web search for that before my appointment, it sounded painful!

I arrived at Immortal Art Studio and waited for Richard to set up his workstation. It was good to see how hygienic everything was, this was very important for me to know. Soon the session started, and I began experiencing being tattooed for the first time. It is a strange and unique feeling; I once heard it described as like being nibbled by an electric squirrel! It was uncomfortable at first, but once the endorphins kicked in it was quite bearable. Richard's energy and unique view on life certainly kept me distracted. A short five hours later and I had my first two bird species tattooed onto my right arm, Red-fronted Serin and Dead Sea Sparrow. A great start, and so I booked my second session for two weeks' time.

During the tattooing phase of my project, I was also promoting what I was doing through talks to local bird clubs, wildlife conservation organisations and educational institutions around Britain. I was traveling away from home a great deal, but I did meet some fantastic people in the process. I was always really nervous before giving a talk, but once I got started, I really enjoyed it. More importantly they usually were well received, and I was able to raise additional funds for Doğa Derneği. Despite finding interaction with new people difficult throughout most of my life, I really enjoyed taking my story around the country. I am not sure when this shift occurred, but perhaps it could have been once my project gathered momentum and people were valuing what I was doing. Of course, it could equally be just a bit of narcissism!

I continued attending tattoo sessions every two weeks, adding to my collection of Turkish bird tattoos, and they were looking fantastic. I also found myself getting increasingly immersed into tattoo culture. This was a quite different world to the one I was familiar with, but I was fascinated by it, and I was beginning to feel like I really fitted in. Tattoo and body modification culture could be described as alternative culture because it challenges the societal norms, though nowadays those borders have got less defined. This subculture oozes creativity, this is what makes it so special and important.

I was spending more time at Immortal Art Studio and rarely thinking about anything else. I opted to have the back of my hands tattooed as well as my arms. Some might suggest that this was not my cleverest move, there is still a stigma attached to visible tattoos. Looking back however, I do not think the rationality part of my brain was working! The birds tattooed on my hands were Radde's Accentor and White- throated Robin, both species that held significant memories for me. During the tattoo process this far, I discovered that most of the skin on the arm felt reasonable when being tattooed, the elbow and fingers though, were a bit nippy!

Having experienced birding abroad, my outlook on birding in the UK had changed a little. I was starting to twitch less and quite content working my way through the complexities of gull identification and any subspecies of any type of bird I saw.

This was all really following on from the International Gull Conference at Peterhead. My Turkish birds' sleeves were just about finished, and I was very pleased with the outcome. I managed to get another tattoo on my right leg from artist Paul Smith at Liverpool Tattoo Convention when I attended with my mother. I managed to book Paul for another leg tattoo at the Northeast Tattoo Convention at Stockton-on-Tees. Shannon and my mum accompanied me for this event. It was very much a family convention, with plenty for children to do. That said, Shannon seemed very content watching me being tattooed for hours on end!

I had started doing a little work at Immortal Art Studio, running their blog, not for money, but in exchange for tattoos of course! I really enjoyed doing this and it paid for me to get some additional tattoos on my neck, legs, and head. I can categorically say that for me the most uncomfortable place to be tattooed is the side of my head, particularly around the temple region. Richard and Rob invited me to a couple of tattoo conventions, one in London and the other was somewhere near Birmingham. Rob is an accomplished artist and has a real skill for realism black and grey tattoos. So, I was very happy with the tattoo he created on me at the earlier convention. Richard is a good all-rounder, but he creates his best work when he has the freedom to let his imagination loose.

During the London tattoo convention, I was the canvas for one of Richard's free reign projects. This involved getting tattooed on my left leg for two consecutive days. I definitely wouldn't recommend this; the second day was horrific! Back at the studio, Richard also created an interesting tattoo onto my left shin, this is a politically charged piece of art with a strong link to Türkiye.

If you remember the various uprisings in the Middle East and North Africa that was dubbed the 'Arab Spring,' then you may remember what happened in Türkiye at the same time. My understanding is that large scale protests across parts of Türkiye, were a reaction to how protesters against environmental damage to Gezi Park in Istanbul were treated by overzealous police. Their tents were set on fire! As the protests spread the title of Gil Scott-Heron's poem 'the revolution will not be televised' seemed worryingly relevant. Instead of covering the uprising on state television, documentaries about penguin's were shown instead. The government used the word Çapulcu to describe the protesters to try and dehumanise the population. Çapulcu roughly translates as marauder or hooligan.

Turkish people in my experience tend to be quite creative, this situation was no exception. They disarmed the word Çapulcu by

115

owning it and the penguin, with a gas mask (due to broad teargas usage) became the iconic symbol of their protest. I had quite a few friends in Türkiye, many who were involved. In fact, one of them phoned me after observing and filming some police brutality. He was quite frightened for his own safety and asked if I would upload his video to YouTube. In addition to that, I decided to get a huge gas masked penguin on my shin in solidarity. I must admit, I made sure I wasn't wearing shorts the next time I crossed the Turkish border!

Charlie told me about a new conservation project that was organised by Ceri Levy. If you are a fan of the Britpop band Blur or Damon Albarn's later creation, Gorillaz, then you may have heard of them. Ceri is a filmmaker who directed films on both these iconic groups. The conservation project that Ceri was involved with, was called 'Ghosts of Gone Birds' and it was using art that largely represented extinct species to raise funds for conservation and awareness of species that were under threat. I liked the idea behind this project as I could see some similarities with what I was trying to achieve. This was a project I really wanted to get involved with, not just because a bit of cross pollination would be potentially good for what I was doing, but also because it was an exciting idea.

I emailed Ceri, introducing him to 'Giving my Right Arm' and describing my proposition. I suggested that I could offer up a bit of chest real estate to have a replica of a piece of art from a 'ghosts' contributor tattooed onto me. Having not heard from Ceri for a few days, I thought, fair enough, that might have been the most ridiculous email he had ever received! However, a week or so later, I got a message from Ceri, containing a fantastic piece of artwork by Ralph Steadman. The artwork entitled 'Kelaynak,' featured the hugely charismatic Northern Bald Ibis, Kelaynak is the Turkish name for the species. I loved the interpretation; I thought Ralph had captured the character of this species superbly. I was sold! I let

Ceri know I was on board and assuming Ralph was happy for me to use his art for my tattoo, we could go ahead as soon as possible. Ceri was keen to come up and film the process for a related documentary he was making. So, after discussing plans with Richard, the date was set.

It was really good to meet Ceri, such a nice person and really passionate about wildlife conservation. As expected, Richard did an amazing job of my tattoo. I loved it then and I love it now! A couple of months later and the Ghosts of Gone Birds art exhibition was about to go live. I was extremely excited to have been invited to the launch. I stayed with Charlie and his partner the night before and then we travelled to the venue in London. When I walked through the door, I had the surreal realisation that for all intents and purposes I was an exhibit!

The exhibition was incredible, there was artwork from the likes of Bruce Pearson, Dafila Scott, Margaret Atwood, Peter Blake and of course Ralph Steadman, and many more besides. It was fantastic to finally meet Ralph, he is such a warm human being. I am not entirely sure what he thought about me, but he did donate to my fundraiser. I also got to meet Jimi Goodwin who is the vocalist, guitarist, and bassist in The Doves. I had been a fan of his band for a while, so I was really pleased to hear of his involvement with 'Ghosts.' He was a genuinely nice guy and an absolute pleasure to chat to. The whole event had been overwhelming, I was so honoured to have been invited. What an experience. Ceri and Ralph went on to author a book about Ralph's huge contribution to Ghosts of Gone Birds.' When I was sent a copy, I was really pleased to see that I had got a mention.

After my mood had been elevated for quite some time, it started to free fall. The hyper enthusiastic, motivated version of me was struggling even to put on a positive facia. The dark numb cloud had returned, and it was horrible.

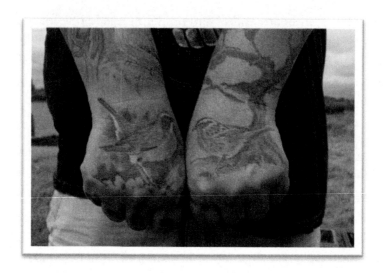

White-throated Robin & Radde's Accentor –My hand tattoos

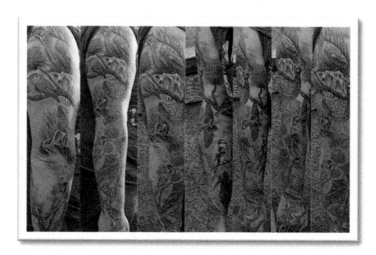

My right arm tattoos.

My left arm tattoo sleeve

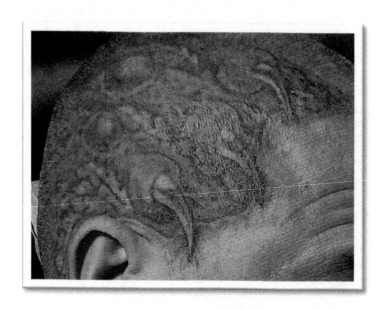

My head tattoo

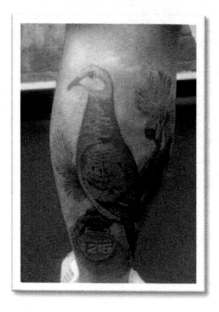

Passenger Pigeon Tattoo

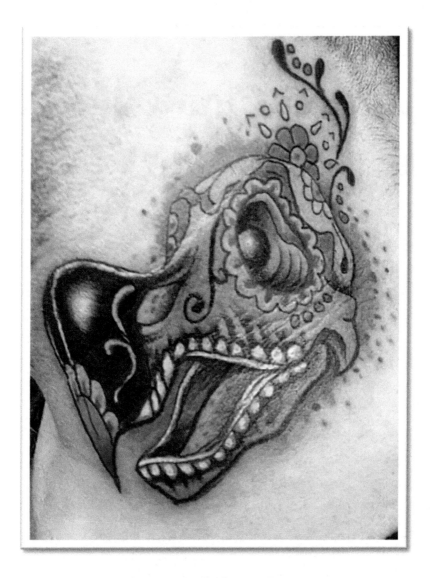

Dodo Sugar Skull – Neck tattoo

Act Six

You don't look like an ultrarunner!

Kath made the short trip into Chances Park for the inaugural Carlisle Parkrun and really enjoyed the experience. This got me thinking, could I, at twenty-two stone (144 kg) in weight, propel myself around the 3.1 miles (5k) of the parkrun course? It seemed like a good goal to aim for. At that point I was very apprehensive about trying to run outside, I thought I would get laughed at because of my size and how slow I would be running. I decided to build up my mileage gradually on the treadmill that I had bought Kath during a previous spending spree. After a few weeks, I had hit my distance target. It was time to see what I was capable.

My friend Sam agreed to accompany me for my first attempt at a parkrun. When we arrived, I could see there was a great mix of people and I felt less out of place than I had expected to! It was very evident though, that I was the only one dressed in a t-shirt and combat shorts with walking boots on my feet! Once the run started, I was quickly reminded that running is hard and running on a treadmill does not prepare you for anything! I did get around in one piece and I enjoyed it in a masochistic sort of way. Something I had not anticipated was how supportive everyone was, I do not just mean Kath and Sam, I mean the marshals, spectators, and the other runners. This was a revelation to me and something I could get used to. I continued participating in parkrun with some regularity and my times gradually came down. I was never going to be superfast, but I was pretty happy when, at my quickest, I ran the five kilometres in around twenty-four minutes.

Running had become a significant part of my life, I joined a local running club in Carlisle, and I began to run regularly with them. I even ran in a few local road races. Well, quite a few actually, they included the Isel Cross, Longtown 10 miler, Carlisle Tri Club 10k and Keswick 'round the houses 10k. I also got my first experience of participating in a trail race. The event was the Karrimor Great Trail Challenge and I opted for the 22k version. It was both brutal and beautiful.

If you remember the tattoo convention I went to in Stockton on Tees, that I mentioned previously; what I did not tell you was that the main purpose was to raise funds and awareness for a family bereavement charity, The founder of the charity asked me if I would join his team running a relay of the Sunderland Marathon. This was quite a big event, so quite exciting for me. I made my way to my start point on the route and waited for the team member running before me to come into the changeover zone, then it was time for me to run. It was a very well supported event, so the atmosphere was fantastic. The 10k of the relay that I was responsible for seemed to flyby. I mean not actually; it took me nearly an hour! I enjoyed it though; this running thing could actually be good for me. It was special to see Kathleen and our girls, when I picked up my medal from the Stadium of Light. Was this where I began convincing myself, I had another marathon in me?

A week or so after my return from Georgia, Kath and I were traveling to Gateshead for the Great North Run. This would be my first road half-marathon and I had picked the biggest half in the world for my debut! We arrived a few hours before the race started,

123

so we could soak up the atmosphere. There were thousands of eager runners getting ready for the challenge ahead of all of us. Soon Kath and I were saying our goodbyes and good lucks as we parted company and went to our respective starting pens (I was in the slow one). It wasn't long before the race started, and I was on my way. The support from the spectators all along the route was fantastic, you can't beat that famous northeast hospitality.

I had not really been able to train for this race properly, but I felt pretty good most of the way to the finish. Perhaps spending a few days at altitude in the High Caucasus had helped with my cardiovascular fitness. It was fantastic seeing Kath in the finish area, she'd had a great run too.

A few weeks after the Great North Run, I participated in my second road half-marathon, The Great Cumbrian Run. A comparatively lower key event, but still with great support from spectators and fellow runners. My running was improving, and I ran that half-marathon an impressive nine minutes quicker than I had run the Great North Run. I was incredibly happy with that result!

The following month or so, I filled my time with a family stuff, a little ecological consultancy work, continuing travelling to various parts of the UK to present my talks and a fair bit of running as and when time allowed. Earlier in the year, (inspired by Kath running the Coniston Trail Marathon) I had entered the ballot for the London Marathon and then promptly forgotten about it. Roll on to late October and I received a London Marathon magazine with 'you're in' on the front cover. I'd actually got a place on the next iteration of the famous race! Okay, I should say that me and the London Marathon have a little bit of history. Six years previously for reasons I really don't know, I tried to get a charity place with Save the Rhino but failed (or so I thought). This seemed like it was a close shave, I hadn't actually run since I was at school. What was I thinking? Around four weeks before London Marathon, I received a call from Save the Rhino informing me that one of their runners had been injured and so they asked me if I would take his place in the race. As I do not have the best relationship with rationality, I accepted. I managed three training runs before the event, with the longest run being somewhere around nine miles. I definitely was not prepared at all!

I did make it to the start line and began the race. I ran where I could and walked where I couldn't. The amazing crowd support kept me going, but it was tough. I was approaching Tower Bridge when I had a bit of a wobble, but after speaking to Kath, I got the encouragement I needed to continue. I was determined to keep going until the marshals stopped me, or I crossed that finish line. Despite having to dodge some drunk people fighting on the course in front of me, I soon found myself running down the Mal and crossing the finish line. I was very proud of what I had achieved, and I felt that I had learnt a lot about myself. With all that said, it took me around six years before I would run again.

The day I got the positive news on my London Marathon place for 2014, I was traveling down to Sheffield to present my 'giving my right arm' talk to Sheffield Bird Study Group. Whilst on the coach traveling southeast, I had a thought, I mused that most runners could run a marathon, so why don't I run fourteen marathons in 2014. Irrational I know, but it was certainly catchy!

Although I would dip in and out of significant depression, this period was dominated by elevated mood. This was certainly fuelled by my talks schedule and the attention this attracted. I was oblivious to this at the time though.

By the time I returned home from Sheffield, I had put a plan together for my marathons project. The charity I was going to raise funds and awareness for, was, Operation Turtle Dove. This was a charity that was working hard to increase the population of nesting Turtle Doves in the UK. My attention was drawn to this organisation by my friend Jonny Rankin, who has been (and still is) raising money for the charity by carrying out some amazing feats of endurance, such as walking across Spain!

The Turtle Dove is a species familiar to most, particularly because it is mentioned in the traditional festive song 'the twelve days of Christmas.' They have declined by around 98% in the UK since the 1970's (c30% in Europe) and are under a real threat of extinction. The main cause of decline is overhunting and habitat loss. This story has some familiarity about it unfortunately. There was a species of pigeon found in North America in unbelievable numbers, observation at the time estimated that flocks over a million strong were frequently seen. This was the commonest bird in North America, with a population estimate between 3 and 5 billion.

The species was the Passenger Pigeon. Unfortunately, the Passenger Pigeon was pushed to extinction in the wild in a relatively short space of time, through unmonitored hunting and habitat loss. There was a clear and obvious familiarity between the dramatic decline of the Turtle Dove and the industrial extermination of the Passenger Pigeon, so I was determined to do what I could to raise awareness of the Turtle Doves plight and raise much needed funds for Operation Turtle Dove's habitat restoration projects. 2014 marked 100 years since the very last Passenger Pigeon on the planet died. She was housed in Cincinnati Zoo in Ohio and her name was Martha.

The title of my campaign was '1000 miles in memory of Martha'. It was important to commemorate Martha as this was a very tragic lesson that was vital for us to learn from. My plan was to run fourteen marathons (or marathon distances) during 2014 and run a minimum of 1000 miles during the 12 months (miles included marathons and training runs) I had a plan in place, so without hesitation (or discussion with anyone) I publicised my plans. There was no going back now! For me, this was an extremely ambitious challenge, and I had no idea if I would succeed. I was going to give it my best shot though.

I closed the year out with a little bit of not particularly well-thought-out training and a few early-winter races including the Ulverston Xmas pudding 10k. I was excited about my running plans for the approaching year and to my surprise, not in the slightest bit nervous!

Birding was still a high priority for me, though looking back, it seems that I was becoming less active in that area. Because I had spent a little time watching birds overseas, I was less inclined to travel distances in Britain to see species I had seen in other countries. Some of the additional stand out species that I did see in the Britain during 2014 were Stilt Sandpiper, Wryneck and Blue-winged Teal. Perhaps the rarest was my second and the Britain's third Masked Shrike, back at the very familiar location of Kilnsea, situated close to Spurn.

Running was really beginning to take priority over my birding. After some sporadic and less than ideal training, I was lining up for my first ever trail marathon. This was the Montane Trail 26 at Grizedale Forest in my adopted county of Cumbria. Whilst waiting to start, I got chatting to a few interesting folks, including a man who was attempting to run fifty marathons, in what was his fiftieth year. That was an incredible challenge, I really hope he succeeded.

It was early February, in the Lake District, so damp and windy conditions were easily predicted. As we set off and began the first climb, I was already questioning my life choices. I knew this was going to be a yomp, but once I had warmed up, I really started to enjoy myself.

Something I had to get used to with trail marathons was having to carry kit. For this race, I had to carry a fully waterproof jacket, first aid kit, bivy bag, hat and gloves, whistle, emergency food and water.

That seemed like a lot to carry, but you do get used to it. Besides, when you are running in remote areas on technical terrain, safety must be a priority.

Loop one of the route was quite nice running, mostly on forest tracks, quite hilly though! This loop stays within the forest, running parallel with Coniston Water, giving spectacular views. As well as the marathon, there was also a half-marathon running at the same time, these participants had to complete the first loop. This meant that there was a fantastic mix of people to engage with as you continued of through the course. The end of loop one ended near the start and then, for marathoners it was time join the second loop. That second loop was particularly challenging, with much more climbing than the previous and the terrain was a lot more varied. This loop took me out of the forest and down to Esthwaite Water and Lake Windermere before climbing up and over Claife Heights. It was an extremely tough race, but an amazing experience and it was such a fantastic feeling crossing that finish line. I was pleased with what I had achieved, and it was made all the sweeter when I saw Kathleen and our girls cheering me on at the finish. One marathon distance done (phew) and only thirteen to go!

Running in 2014, wasn't just about the marathons, it was also about my accumulative distance, working towards that 1000-mile total. To help make this achievable and to add to my training miles, I also entered some shorter events. The first of these events was the stunning Haweswater Half-marathon organised by local running club, Eden Runners.

The race starts in the village of Bampton and follows the road that hugs the southeast edge of Haweswater in its entirety before turning around in the far end carpark and returning to Bampton. It was a wet day; in fact, it was either raining or sleeting the whole way around. The first climb out of the village was brutal and it was very undulating after that, before a nice downhill finish. The views made the challenging work worthwhile, this had to be the most scenic road half marathons I'd ever done. With an elevation gain of 1,472 feet (449 metres) this was the hilliest half I had participated in, despite this, with a finishing time of 2.19.23, this was my fastest half-marathon event so far. It was another fantastic inclusive event in a beautiful part of the world with great support from marshals, runners, and spectators.

Still a little tired, yet hyped from Haweswater, I was participating in another road race the following weekend. This time it was the Dentdale 14. This race started in the Cumbrian village of Dent and follows a narrow loop of Dentdale. Dent lies within the historical boundary of the West Riding of Yorkshire. The whole valley is contained within the Yorkshire Dales National Park. Suffice to say, it was a very scenic route. Not surprisingly it was also quite a tough route (aren't they all?), particularly on my tired legs and other such excuses. It was nice to get another race ticked off and more miles on the tally.

My next event was the Sport in Action Longtown 10 miler, the same event that I ran for the first time the previous year. This time, the race went well, and I really enjoyed it (even that monster hill!) and I even got a nice ego boost when I crossed the finish line a very tasty twelve minutes quicker than my previous attempt.

The question marathon runners frequently get asked when talking to others about marathons is 'how far is that marathon.' For some reason, some people can comprehend that the London Marathon is 26.2 miles, but any other marathon event is open season for confusion. All marathon distances are 26.2 miles, although trail marathons can sometimes be a little less or as is usual, a bit more. This is generally because it is quite difficult to accurately measure a course on trail, compared to road.

About seven weeks later, I had my next marathon race to take on. Billed as the world's biggest marathon, it was of course the London Marathon. As I mentioned earlier in this chapter, I had previous experience of this event. My last attempt was pretty horrific, and I crossed the finish line in a very pedestrian 7.05.50. I certainly had not trained well enough to be planning on chasing personal bests, but I did hope I would be able to run this race a little faster.

The main plan of course, was to get around in one piece. I knew I could do the distance, I just had to make sure I crossed that finish line. I'd booked myself into some budget accommodation, which turned out to be in Forest Gate. This was fascinating to me, because I had only previously heard of Forest Gate from a track on Plan B's seminal debut album 'who needs actions when you got words' titled 'Rakin' the dead.' He did not paint the best of pictures, but it was alright.

Prior to arriving at Forest Gate, I visited the London Marathon expo at the ExCel close to Victoria Dock. Once I'd registered for the race and collected my bib number, I had a little wander around the expo before returning to my accommodation. After eating some food and making sure I was well hydrated, I had an early night. I did not get a lot of sleep as the hotel owners kids decided to rev their hot hatch engines most of the night, I couldn't close my window because the whole hotel reeked of cigarette smoke. Not the start for which I was hoping!

After breakfasting, I jumped onto the train to Marble Arch and made my way to the start area. There was a huge amount of people, all nervously waiting to begin this iconic race. Being more of a country-boy, I must admit finding the masses a little bit daunting. That said, it was incredible to realise that all these people would be taking on the same challenge as me, but for a plethora of reasons that would be personal to them. Once the race started, I was a little taken aback by the heat, it was more than 20 degrees Celsius (68 degrees Fahrenheit), not the April temperatures in which I had trained. This was going to be a tough day out!

I just plodded it out and did the best I could. The masses of runners and supporters along the whole route of the marathon are spectacular and do, for most, make this a special experience. For someone with a diagnosis of both general anxiety disorder and social anxiety disorder, this added more difficulty to an already challenging day. I decided I just had to keep my focus on the end goal and keep plodding on. I went through periods of enjoyment and periods of quiet despair at alternating frequencies. Just another day at the office! In the last five or six miles I found myself chatting to an interesting individual, he was professional skateboarder, Ben Cundall. At this point we were both struggling with the distance, so we stuck together giving encouragement where needed. It was an amazing feeling running down the Mal and then over the finish line. I will be forever grateful and appreciative to Ben for his company in those last miles. I crossed the finish line in 6.00.30. Not a fantastically quick time, but still over an hour faster than my previous attempt. That was marathon distance number two of fourteen done, just another twelve left to do, Easy, right?

Just a few weeks after London Marathon, I was attempting the Stratford Rotary Shakespeare Marathon. It was another long journey for this one, but this time Kathleen and our girls were traveling down to support me. This was a nice smaller scale event, compared to London and it was set up purely to raise vital funds for charities. The marathon and half marathon started at the same time, so there was a nice mix of runners. The route took me around the historical Stratford upon Avon before looping around some pleasant countryside. The half-marathoners veered off back towards the town near the end of the Stratford Greenway. I was sorely tempted to join them at this point but knuckled down and continued along the full marathon course. My run was going well up until about mile nineteen when the wheels started to buckle. I was officially in the pain cave, time to embrace the discomfort and keep moving on. It was style it out time! The last seven miles or so, were a big challenge.

When you are physically done and mentally broken, this is the time when the support of other runners and spectators really holds a lot of power. Those interactions coupled with knowing my girls were waiting on the finish line for me. really spurred me on. I crossed the finish line in 4.58.33. I was very tired, but ecstatic with my time. I had run this marathon over an hour quicker than me previous fastest marathon. Getting to share this with my family was really special.

Three marathon distances done, just eleven left to do... The following weekend back in Keswick and I was lining up to start the Keswick Half-marathon. The route circumnavigates Derwent Water with an extra little loop near Newlands Hause. With over 1,300 feet (396 meters) of elevation, this was a tough and hilly road race. It was another one of those races where the hard graft was rewarded by incredible views. Still on a high from the Shakespeare Marathon I was incredibly happy to have finished this event in 2.13.23. I think, at the time that this was the fastest I'd ran a half-marathon race in. What was happening? Somehow, I was beginning to improve. .

Kathleen had reinvented herself as a fell runner and her enthusiasm for this flavour of running had begun to rub off on me. Although there are no true wild areas remaining in the UK, fell running is probably the one true discipline of running where you really feel engaged with the wilderness. We were frequently testing ourselves on some of the lake district mountains, often with Sam. This was always an amazing experience whatever the weather and it was the nursery grounds for more outlandish adventures.

The next marathon on the schedule was the Brathay Windermere Marathon. This race is billed as the UK's most scenic marathon, although it is undoubtedly very scenic, there are a few stunningly scenic trail marathons that could claim that lay claim to that crown. Scenery is never cheap and with over 1,700 feet (518 meters) of elevation gain, this promised to be a toughie. This marathon was first run in 1982 and was continued for only four years, until it was successfully revived in 2007 by the Brathay Trust. Although the Brathay Trust do organise and run quite a few nice running events in the Windermere area, they are firstly and foremost a charity. The charity was set up to help empower young people and families from Cumbria and Yorkshire through wellbeing and self-development initiatives. A very worthy charity and it is fantastic that the fell running legend, Joss Naylor is a long-time supporter of the trust.

It was the morning of the race, and it was a hot one! The race is started by the sound of a local gamekeeper firing his shotgun into the air. I personally found this tradition in poor taste. I'm sure many will see the ceremony as quaint, but it really isn't. There is something deeply wrong with a society that normalises the unnecessary killing of animals for fun. Perhaps that's just me though, but it certainly the reason why I've only ran this particular event once. After I had calmed my frustrated mind, I got into my stride and allowed myself to enjoy where I was. The scenery was breathtaking and nicely varied as I ran anticlockwise around Lake Windermere. A mixture of warm temperatures and a hilly route made this a very challenging run . I did meet some lovely folk during the race and the spectator support was amazing. It was fantastic to cross the finish line in an expectedly steady 5.29.00. Not my quickest, but certainly not my slowest, I'll take that! I had enjoyed the marathon and it felt good to say four done, ten to go!

The following weekend I was lining up for my second Montane Trail 26 event of the year, the Howgills Marathon. This one was absolutely brutal. The race started in the village of Sedbergh and once through the village it was a sharp unrelenting climb up onto the Howgills. The route was expectedly hilly with over 3,700 feet (1,127 meters) of elevation gain. I was questioning my capabilities on many occasions during this race. I can vouch for the fact that seven days between tough marathons is not enough time to recover! All excuses aside, the run back along the river was lovely, the last sneaky steep climb, not so much! I crossed the very welcome finish line in a time of 7.15.23, both my slowest marathon time and hardest marathon race at that time. I really didn't care about the time; I was just happy to have finished it and for the amazing experience. It was nice to have Kathleen and Sam cheering me at the finish, they had both taken on the half-marathon race and they'd had great runs. That was marathon number five done and dusted, just nine remaining. It was a good feeling to be into single figures.

I knew at this point that I had bitten off more than I could chew, so it was just as well I didn't have anything bigger planned... Looking back on my races from 2014, I can clearly see that I put absolutely no thought into my recovery or capability, I had an idea and just ran with it. For some reason I thought after the difficulty of Howgills, I would be fine to race in a road 10k just ten days later. Well, as it happens this worked out far better than it should have. I ran the Carlisle 10k race in just over 52 minutes, which at the time was a very unexpected personal best.

All I can say is that I must be invincible, I really felt like I was. 'No Tristan, you're really not,' was what my inner dialogue shouted at me during my next marathon attempt. The event was the High Terrain Events Scafell Pike Marathon. The name of the event should tell you all you need to know about the difficulty level of this one. I had checked out the mountain section of the route earlier in the month, so I did know what I was taking on. Once I started running, I knew something was not right with me, I had no energy and just felt unwell. I plodded on until I reached the checkpoint just before the mountain section (at around mile 13). I knew it was not sensible for me to continue, the last thing I wanted to do was put myself and potentially others (mountain rescue etc) at risk. So, I had to do the sensible thing and withdraw from the race. I was very disappointed in myself; it wasn't good to have my first DNF (did not finish).

With my mood being consistently elevated for the previous few months, the cracks were starting to show, and my mood was in free fall. The following couple of weeks I knew I had to rest up as I had my biggest running challenge to take on next. My mental health was really suffering now, but I had to force it into superficial hiding because I had made a public declaration to run these ridiculous challenges for Operation Turtle Dove and I wasn't prepared to let anyone down.

My next marathon was, well it was three marathon plus distances over three consecutive days. I must admit, this wasn't my best plan following my Scafell Pike Marathon failure, but it was what it was! Thankfully, I would have company for this adventure as Sam was running with me.

The Hadrian's Wall path runs from Wallsend east of Newcastle to Bowness-on-Solway in Cumbria and is 84 miles in distance. Most people walk it from the Solway to Newcastle for some reason, we were contrary of course, starting in Wallsend and finishing in Bowness-on-Solway, this direction just made more sense to us!

Sam's wife, Samantha, kindly took us over to Wallsend early on the first day of this adventure. You should realise by now that I do not run my life in a slick organised fashion and this adventure was going to be no different. We set of for day one of our Hadrian's Wall challenge and things were feeling good. However, we eventually realised we had set off in the wrong direction. Back at Wallsend with a few unnecessary miles already ran, we asked a Roman soldier for directions. To be fair, I don't know if he was a real Roman soldier, but he was definitely dressed like one! So, take two and we were properly off on our adventure. The run along the River Tyne into Newcastle and on to Ryton was quite pleasant, though even at that early stage, I had low energy and was struggling.

I just had to plod it out. We continued and got ourselves out of the urban zones and into some nice countryside.

The climb up to Heddon-on-the-Wall was a bit tasty, but fifteen miles in and we were doing okay given the circumstances. We briefly stopped to get some snacks and so Sam could do some pre-emptive patching up of his feet. Then we continued on our way again. It was nice being out of the city and up onto higher ground, but I was struggling.

My pace was slowing further, and we were beginning to get a little concerned that we wouldn't get to our accommodation in time for a much-needed evening meal. By the time we reached Whittle Dene Reservoir we made the decision that Sam, being fitter and faster than me, would run on to get our meal ordered before the kitchen closed. I continued along the Hadrian's Wall path at my own pace, the route was running parallel to the old military road and seemed to go on forever. I was in a dark place and really finding things extremely challenging. I was questioning everything, and my inner dialogue was telling me some home truths that were very unhelpful to hear. I just kept moving and hoped for the best.

The last hour or so was in the dark which added to the difficulty, but it felt good to reach the finish of day one. That was one hell of first day of the adventure and we had run 33.1 miles, this put us clearly in ultra distance territory and it was the longest I'd ever ran in one go. It was great to see Sam sat in the bar with a pint waiting for me and although I was not feeling hungry in the slightest, I forced some food down. This would hopefully give me a bit of a chance for the following day. I cannot dress it up any other way, day one was, for me, horrendous with very few positives. I was just hoping the next few days would be a vast improvement...

On our way through to Wallsend the previous morning with Samantha, we had dropped our overnight gear off at the hotel in Wall. So, once breakfasted on the morning of stage two, we were met by Kathleen and my girls, who picked up our night gear and dropped off some supplies for the day ahead. It was so good to see them and just the boost I desperately needed.

As Sam and I set off for day two, I had a different mind-set than the previous day. We knew that this stage of the route would be the toughest technically, but it was also the most scenic. Our game plan was to take it steady and enjoy the views. Easy, right? The first few miles were tough, my legs were quite sore from the previous days' effort, but I just had to accept the discomfort and enjoy the views. It was going to be a pain cave sort of day! Surprisingly, my mind felt quite good, so I was enjoying chatting with Sam and the soaking in the amazing views. This had the makings of a good day! We ran from Wall, past Chollerford then back to shadowing the old military road.

We passed some interesting historical or scenic sites such as the Housesteads Roman Fort, Broomlee Lough, Vindolanda, Greenlee Lough, Crag Lough, Cawfield Lough, Sycamore Gap, Gilsand and Birdoswald. We finished the day at Banks East Turret having enjoyed most of the 26.7 miles covered. Although this day was not without its challenges, I really enjoyed the journey.

My head was back in the game! Day three was very much our victory lap, running on mostly familiar territory. We set off from Banks East Turret and both of us were feeling the strain of the previous couple of days. It was nice to start the day with a descent off the higher ground and towards the river Eden. Despite it being mostly flat, the run into Carlisle was quite tough going. We were obviously both very tired and Sam was having painful issues with his feet. We made a strategic pit stop at the Sands Centre, so Sam could try and sort his feet out. We also took the opportunity to grab some food (and a pint for Sam of course) before tackling the final fourteen miles of the route.

It was a nice run into Grinsdale along the river and we were soon dropping towards the Solway Firth. I was feeling stronger and stronger and for the first time I was ahead of Sam, this was not normal! I was running on adrenaline at this point! Sam wasn't slowing due to fitness problems; he was slowing because he was in agony due to shredded feet. We both kept going the best we could, and the miles trickled past us. It was an amazing feeling running shoulder to shoulder with Sam into Bowness-on-Solway to the finish of our incredible three-day adventure.

Day three was complete and that was another 28.5 miles run. That was a total of 88.3 miles covered over the three consecutive days! When we turned the corner into the finish it was quite emotional being met by our respective partners and kids, Sam's children had even made a lovely banner to congratulate us on our achievement. Sam's brother, Matt, put an ice-cold bottle of beer in our hands. This remains the most satisfying beer I've ever had! Running the full length of Hadrian's Wall had been an incredible experience and something that I am still immensely proud of to this day. Sharing the adventure with Sam, was amazing. I am very confident when I say that I would not have achieved this without him. That was marathon distances six, seven and eight completed, just six more to go. Will I ever learn? History suggests no!

Just seven days after completion of the Hadrian's Wall challenge I was stood at the start line in quite hot conditions for the Lakeland Trails Marathon at Coniston Water. This was going to be interesting! My legs were still feeling battered from Hadrian's Wall, and I was still understandably tired. Within the first few miles I knew it was going to be one of those all too familiar pain cave days. When you're running this route on a beautiful day, you can't help but smile to yourself. I was not very comfortable, but the scenery was so stunning, so it was difficult for me to feel too sorry for myself. It was a case of enjoying the views whilst continuing to plod forwards. Much as I enjoyed the scenery, I was very relieved to cross that finish line. Marathon number nine completed in 6.41.29, I was quite happy with that considering what I had been putting my body through.

As part of my raising awareness of the plight of the Turtle Dove I collaborated with Mark Avery to give my '1000 miles in memory of Martha' talk. Mark Avery is an author, blogger and former director of conservation at the RSPB. Mark is at the forefront of avian conservation activism. He had just published his book 'A Message from Martha – The extinction of the Passenger Pigeon and its relevance today.' This seemed like a good opportunity for us to work together. I spoke to Mark and told him about my project and suggested we could link our two approaches for the greater good. He agreed and invited me to join him at his prime lecture spot at the British Birdwatching Fair.

I travelled down to the bird fair with my eldest daughter, Shannon. We were camping close to the bird fair; camping would be a new experience for Shannon. We spent what remained of the day at the fair, catching up with a few familiar faces and checking out some of the marquees. It was fantastic to meet up with my friend Gunnar. He is a Swede who has lived in Peru for many years, he runs his own bird tour company from there. In addition to that, Gunnar is an accomplished singer and musician and a very decent marathon runner. He had arranged a little run with a local running club for the following morning, both Shannon and I were also going to tag along. The next morning, we met up for our pre-breakfast run with Gunnar and the group of local runners. It was a nice steady five miles flanking Rutland Water. Shannon was not a very keen runner, but she did brilliantly to keep plodding without any complaints.

We both arrived at the bird fair ready for a decent breakfast. We then continued to meet up with friends and explore the marquees. I had an appointment with a publisher about the possibility of getting a deal for a book idea about my 'giving my right arm for

Turkish wildlife' project. I was a little unsure about this as when I spoke to them the previous year, they seemed more interest in my twitter following (which was then quite small) than my book idea. This year, however. because I had a decent enough twitter following (c10,000+), they were showing interest. The meeting went well, and we agreed terms.

The book content was restricted to keep the format more in line with the publishing company theme, but I was prepared to compromise as it was a story important enough to share. Unfortunately, I never authored the book in the end, after I became very ill, I moved on from the publisher.

After my appointment, I met up with Mark Avery and we prepared for our talk. I was quite nervous, but Mark gave me positive encouragement which helped me settle my nerves. The talk went well, and the audience was brilliantly engaging. When I saw the emotion shown by some members, it struck me how much the loss of birds such as the Turtle Dove would impact on people's lives. This was something I would think about during my remaining miles.

Just a couple of weeks after my return from bird fair, I found myself nervously in the starting area for my first official ultra marathon race. The race was the St Bega's Ultra 35 (SBU35), an event organised by UKanTrail. This was a race that was described as suitable for beginner and experienced ultra trail runners alike, this sounded like I would have a good chance of survival! The trail started in Dodd Wood, overlooking Bassenthwaite Lake and followed the route that the legendary princess, St Bega was believed to have followed. The course continued from Dodd through the northern Lake District, finishing on the coastal town of St Bee's.

After Kath and our girls dropped me off in the Dodd Wood carpark, I registered for the race and waited nervously for the coach to arrive from St Bee's with most of the other competitors. The race began and of course it was an uphill start! We skirted around the slopes of Dodd looking down towards Bassenthwaite Lake, before a steep and technical descent in the direction of Portinscale on the western edge of Derwentwater. This was all familiar territory for me, but I never tired of the beautiful views.

The trail was flat at this stage as it hugged the edge of the lake before entering the magical Borrowdale Valley. Next there was a short sharp climb around Castle Crag.

Unlike every other trail race I'd participated in, this one was not marked, navigation was solely aided by a 'road book' that contained a detailed written description of the route. This obviously required me to keep paying attention, which was not my strongest attribute. In the Castle Crag area, I got chatting to another runner. Martin had completed the SBU35 previously, so he knew the route reasonably well, he also had a GPS exchange file (GPX) of the full route downloaded to his watch for a backup. This was helpful and meant I could just concentrate on putting one foot in front of the other. Martin was a fascinating guy, and it was great chatting to him as we continued along the route.

We buddied up for the remainder of the ultra-marathon which helped keep me going and stopped me getting lost in in my own head. As we continued through the exquisitely scenic Borrowdale Valley, Martin informed me that he would have to put in is earphones in so he could listen to some 'lord of the rings music,' to make his experience of that section of course that much more dramatic! I thought this was hilarious, though I did like his thinking.

During the biggest climb of the race, up to Honister Slate Mine, I learnt one of the golden rules of trail running. That rule is 'if you see a race photographer, you've got to make you're your running,' nobody wants a commemorative picture of them looking tired and walking do they! Of course, the first race photographer was sat at the top of the biggest climb, well they always are! After the steep relentless climb up to Honister, we were treated to magnificent views of Buttermere and Crummock Water, before the slippery and very technical descent down to the iconic Black Sail Youth Hostel. This was followed by some easier flatter running along the edge of Ennerdale Water.

Once we got off the fell terrain, I was really starting to struggle. The final noteworthy climb of the course up to the summit of Dent Fell, seemed massive and unrelenting. The reality was that compared to the climbs I'd already done; this one was minor. I think the reason I was struggling so much was down to a poor nutrition plan. I was still making all this up as I went along after all.

Once we got up to the top of Dent it was an easy descent down to Cleator, where the final aid station of the race was. We arrived at the aid station, and I was done, I felt like my race was over. The marshals were fantastic, they made me a sugary tea to boost my energy levels and encouraged me to continue. There was only six miles or so left, so now feeling a little more energised I felt able to keep plodding it out. The marshals along the route and in all the aid stations were absolutely amazing. The majority were members of local West Cumbrian running club, The St Bee's Triers.

Those last six miles were tough, but I had fresh determination and was focused on getting the job done. Crossing that finish line felt incredible, seeing Kathleen and our girls cheering me on was beautiful as was the beer put in my hand by the race director! I finished the thirty-six miles, in a little over 11 hours, but I was very proud of what I'd achieved. I could now officially call myself an ultrarunner!

I was super appreciative of Martin's company and support and the support and encouragement of the marshal's and aid station volunteers. Without them, I doubt I would have finished the race.

I should clarify here, what I mean by the term ultra runner and ultra marathon. As stated earlier, a marathon is a foot race over 26.2 miles. An ultra marathon is technically a foot race or distance beyond 26.2 miles. However, the entry level ultra marathon tends to start at the distance of 31miles (50k). Other popular distances are 62 miles (100k), 100 miles (161k) and even 250 miles (402k). It is a whole new subculture too!

Two weeks after SBU35, I was embarking on marathon distance number eleven of the planned fourteen. Because of my DNF at the Scafell Pike Marathon in July, I had to find an alternative. I planned a flat coastal route from Glasson to Silloth. Easy right? Kath dropped me off at Glasson in the cool morning air and I was off. The first hour or so was relatively easy and I was enjoying myself. Things got a bit trickier when the sun got higher, and the temperature rocketed. Kathleen was trying to crew me, although she met me near Newton Arlosh without any water! She did get me some a bit further along the road though.

I must admit I found this route a lot more difficult than I expected. Running distance on the flat can be quite deceptive, you'd assume it would be easy, but you are using the same muscle groups all the time, at least when hills are involved you get to mix it up bit. The miles crawled by, but eventually I was running along the promenade at Silloth, greeted by my cheering family. Solo marathons are tough. That had to be most boring marathon ever! Of course, we know what goes with Silloth, ice-creams! I was tired, thirsty, and very warm, so I was quite pleased to get an Ice-cream from the van by the lifeboat station. However, I do not know what the vendor had done to it, but it tasted awful. It turns out the gulls were not as fussy as me!

With the Glasson to Silloth marathon completed in 5.43.04, I just had three marathons left to do. I was beginning to start believing I might just survive all fourteen!

The following weekend I was down at Stickle Barn ready for the Langdale Marathon. This was a road marathon, but with a lot of stunning scenery. It is a very hilly route, but the first six or seven miles felt good. Unfortunately, at mile seven the proverbial wheels began to fall off. I had picked up a foot injury. The marathon route was two loops of the half marathon course, which was running at the same time. I decided to continue on running the further six miles back to Stickle Barn and reassess things there. Arriving back, I knew I could not continue, so I had to make do with completing the half marathon. With 1,400 feet (427 meters) of elevation gain, this was the hilliest road half marathon I'd achieved, so given the circumstances I was happy enough with a time of 2.33.18. Kath also ran the half, though, thankfully she had a better run than me.

With a bit of forced rest for a week, then a couple of tester road runs and a sneaky fell run up Skiddaw and I was okay to tackle the Great Cumbria Run. The first half went quite well, but the second half, not so much. I'm not sure what was wrong, I knew my foot still wasn't 100%, but I didn't feel great either, I felt like I was going to collapse at one point. Excuses aside, I did finish the race and in a time of 2.10.08, which surprisingly was a personal best for me at the time.

To allow my body some time to rest and recover, I only did a short trail run the following day and nothing until marathon distance number twelve six days later. Because I'm a glutton for punishment, marathon distance number twelve was back on trails and back on the Hadrian's Wall path on the higher ground from Wall to Banks East Turret. I was on my own for this one, so that would certainly add to the challenge. I took it steady as was dictated by the terrain in all honesty, but I really enjoyed the distance. It was nice to be back up on the wall, enjoying those stunning views. I was getting closer, twelve marathons down and just two to go.

All those miles were obviously continuing to take their toll on my body, so I gave myself the full week off from running, before tackling my penultimate marathon distance. I was pleased that Sam was joining me for this one. Our original plan was to run from Banks East Turret to Glasson along the familiar Hadrian's Wall path. However, we soon discovered that we didn't know the route as well as we should've and managed to take a wrong turn in the first mile (surprising, I know, right...)! We were not on the path we had planned, but we did know where we were, so we just continued and made up our route as we went. It was nice to have a little freedom anyway. From Banks East Turret we dropped down into Lanercost, then Brampton before passing through High Crosby, Low Crosby and then followed the River Eden into Carlisle. An interesting route for sure and typically challenging.

Just seven days later and I was travelling down to the city of Leicester with Kathleen, Shannon, Erin and Thea for my fourteenth and final marathon of the year. Once we arrived in Leicester we checked into our hotel and awaited the arrival of friend and fellow Operation Turtle Dove fundraiser, Jonny Rankin. I was happy to have Jonny accompanying for my last marathon of the year, not only because he is fearless fundraising for the same charity and inspired me to take on '1000 miles in memory of Martha', but also because this was going be his very first marathon. It was going to be fantastic to share this experience with him.

The following morning, having both registered, we lined up in the starting area, ready for the off. It was a fantastic atmosphere with a lot of enthusiastic supporters and quite a big field of runners eager to begin their adventure. Kath and my girls cheered us along with everyone else as the race started. Jonny is usually hyped for life, and this time he was definitely on the mega-hyped side of the street. It was going to be one hell of an adventure!

The race route took us on a tour of Leicester City which is quite a pretty city as it happens. The course then took us out of the city into some lovely countryside including King Lear Lake and

Watermead Country Park, before entering the city again. The support around the residential areas was some of the best I had experienced. Passing through a shopping centre at one point in the race was quite unique experience. There were difficulties during the run, as is always expected, but overall, it was a fantastic experience. We were not there to break records or smash pb's, we just wanted to get around and enjoy it. We finished the race in a respectable 5.26.52. Jonny had completed his first Marathon which was incredibly special; and unbelievably, I had run fourteen marathons and over one thousand miles for Operation Turtle Dove, people that look like me, don't run one marathon, let alone fourteen! I had done it though and I was elated.

It was still October, so I was not quite done yet. In fact, the following weekend I ran in the Keswick AC Derwent 10, a tough enough road race that starts at Derwent Close in Keswick, circumnavigates Derwentwater and finishes at Keswick Rugby Club. I really enjoyed this race, running around the lake is fantastic every time. My fitness had improved during the year as I ran the race a pretty impressive eight minutes quicker than the previous year.

A few weeks later I was racing again, another ten miler, this time the Border Harriers Brampton to Carlisle 10. I must admit, although this race has been run for a staggering number of years (65 years by 2014), but it is quite a dull route. It is an immensely popular event however, so perhaps it's just me! I knew what to expect with this one, so I just settled into a rhythm and made my way along the point-to-point route. I managed to finish with a distance personal best, so I felt very happy with that.

I decided to finish the year with a little flourish and run every day in December. Not the most sensible decision, but I rarely make those it seems! I did a mixture of short road runs, trail runs, fell runs and a couple more races. My final two races of the year were quite different. The first was the Hoad Hill Harriers 10k road race in Ulverston. This is quite a nice low-key event, and I was very happy that I managed to complete it with a shiny new 10k pb! My final race of 2014 was quite different to anything I had done throughout the year. It was the NoEgo Headtorch Trail Race in Whinlatter Forest. This was a six-mile trail race in the dark, what could possibly go wrong! It was a cold one, with snow on the ground and I absolutely loved it. What a race to close off the year with.

After my final run, on December 31st, 2014, I had run fourteen marathon distances (including four ultra distances), five half marathon races, three 10-mile races and five 10k or shorter races during the year. My elevation gain for the 12 months was over 100,000 feet (30,480 meters) and my mileage for 2014 was an amazing (for me) 1,206 miles (1,940 kilometres). Not bad for a fat lad! More importantly I managed, by kind donations (by over 100 people), to raise £2,078 for Operation Turtle Dove.

This money was used to create a specially formulated seed mix. This 'turtle dove mix' has been developed by Operation Turtle Dove researchers. It contains early-flowering varieties of plants like vetches and fumitory, which provide turtle doves with much-needed seed food when they arrive in the country after their long migration and to feed their offspring later in the summer. Every £150 raised buys enough seed to cover an area roughly the size of a football pitch with Turtle Dove food. So, 1000 miles in memory of Martha has raised enough money to provide enough habitat to fill an area of nearly fourteen football pitches! That made me incredibly happy indeed.

I learnt a lot about myself through taking on this running challenge. The first realisation was that I go through episodes of making single-minded, big decisions without engaging the rational part of my brain. I do see this as a positive attribute, sometimes. Those decisions can enrich my life. Looking at me, you would agree that I have absolutely no business rocking up to run a marathon or ultra marathon, yet I was able to succeed. What I lack in physique and ability, I make up for in stubbornness. The last thing I realised about myself, was that I'm most comfortable being uncomfortable. This is just as well as there is very little comfort in my mind most of the time!

Whilst I was incredibly proud to have raised a good amount of money for the respective charities with my 'giving my right arm' and '1000 miles in memory of Martha' projects, I did get frustrated with the fact that for the effort and permanence of what I did, the totals raised still felt very low. Perhaps my marketing and fundraising skills were coming up short? I did realise the human recipient charities would always attract more donors than wildlife recipient charities, but it still frustrated me. I felt that I had gone beyond what most people would have done and the charities that I was passionate about deserved much more. I have a regular habit of over analysing myself and this situation was a prime example.

There were moments in my life where I could be described as having delusions of grandeur. At this stage of my existence, I had no idea of the reasons for this behaviour. The questions I asked myself were 'why did I begin these projects?' and 'was it for the attention?' I would be the first to admit that the attention and interactions you can get as a by-product from fundraising projects like mine, is pleasant, but I'd hate to think I would be that narcissistic to go through so much effort for cold hard attention. I certainly recognise that I was very passionate about both the causes I raised money for, and it was that thought that helped through the challenging times. The bottom line is that my expectations are often higher than what is realistic. This is something I seem to replicate in many other areas of my life.

2014 was done and dusted and I was proud of what I had achieved. Running had now become a major part of my life and I wanted to continue this into 2015 and beyond. Having raised much needed funds for Operation Turtle Dove during the previous year, I was keen to follow this vein into 2015.

My plan was to run 2015 miles, which would include twenty marathon or ultra marathon distances. This was a big step up, especially when you consider that the events and distances I was planning to run, included, the Ultimate Trails Challenge 110k Ultra Marathon, Wainwrights Coast to Coast (195 miles in four days), Cumbria Way 110k Ultra Marathon and Hell of a Hill (5 consecutive days of Marathon Running). I was quite confident in my ability then, though some might say delusional! I started the new year running a nice mix of road, trails, and fells as well as a little bit of cross training.

My first race of the year was a revisit of the Sport in Action Resolution 10k, which I managed to run quicker than the previous year, with a respectable time of 53.41. Next up was another familiar route, the Montane Grizedale Trail26 Marathon. With over 5000 feet (1,524 metres) of elevation gain, how could I not remember it! It was as tough as I remembered, but I really enjoyed it, even though I was slower this time. After not much recovery time, it time for me to tackle my first official hill or fell race, the iconic Carnethy 5. The conditions are always interesting at this late winter event in the Pentland Hills, snow would almost be a guarantee. That year's iteration was no different, plus there were fierce winds. There is a traditional fast start to this race, on the flat moorland area before the long steep climb up to Scald Law. One of those climbs that force you to question what the hell you are doing! After Scald Law it was over the top of South Black Hill, before running the ridge of East Kip and West Kip. Next was a nice run down into the valley towards Loganlea Reservoir before the last big climb up to Carnethy. Then a fantastic scree surf down and back to the finish. Certainly, an exhilarating race and without a doubt, the toughest fell run I'd ever participated in.

For something slightly off-piste, I ran in the Mad March Hare obstacle race with Kathleen, her two sisters and friend, Lisa. A few years previously, we had run in the Total Warrior obstacle race at Shap, so we had some idea of what to expect. The Hexham course was definitely more Craggy Island than Total Warrior. Despite it feeling outright dangerous in places, it was really genuine fun, and it was nice to do something a bit different.

I had offered myself up to get a tattoo of a Passenger Pigeon on one of my legs, if my fundraising total exceeded £3,000.00, it didn't, so I put that idea on the back burner. A little while later I was contacted by a production company who were making a documentary series for the Freeview channel Spike (later 5Spike). The title of the series was Tattoo Disasters UK. Not the greatest of titles for someone as proud of their tattoos as I was. The production team reassured me that the format of the episodes was to have a few tattoo disaster stories and one positive tattoo story, they assured me that I would be the positive story.

Now, I was very aware that these types of series try to sensationalise the narrative and make individuals look either extreme, stupid, or extremely stupid! However, I also knew that this was an opportunity to get my conservation fundraising projects to a wider audience. So, I cautiously agreed to take part. The journalist and camera operator arrived at my home and after a bit of an introduction, he set up his kit and began interviewing me. He seemed a decent enough person, but he had the gift of the gab, so I knew I would have to watch myself and how I was being portrayed.

Once we had finished the initial interview, we spent the rest of the day filming at various locations, such as a local nature reserve and Carlisle city centre. I was then asked if they could film me getting a tattoo. This was very short notice, sometimes you have to wait months for an appointment. When I spoke to Richard and explained the situation, he was very accommodating and agreed to come in on his day off to tattoo me. I'd sourced my favourite illustration of a Passenger Pigeon by Hayashi and Toda and one of my recent Montane Trail26 Marathon medals, for Richard to incorporate into the design. Once he had everything set up. the cameras were rolling, and we were ready to go. This was my first tattoo in almost two years, and I must admit it was a bit nippy to begin with, and throughout what was quite a long session. If it had been my first tattoo it may have been my last! Despite that experience, Richard had created a beautiful piece of artwork on the entirety of my right calf.

A few months later 'my episode' of Tattoo Disasters UK was televised, and I was quite happy with the final edit. I felt I had been portrayed fairly, so I didn't come across as too much of an idiot! More importantly my dialogue about my 'giving my right arm for Turkish wildlife' and '1000 miles in memory of Martha' fundraising projects, made the cut! Thankfully, I also got a lot of positive feedback from people who had watched the episode.

The close of March saw me running my second marathon distance of the year, this time with friends, Andrew, and Robert. We were on nicely familiar ground, my favourite section of the Hadrian's Wall path, between Wall and Banks East Turret. A tough old route and the weather threw wind, rain, and hail at us, but it was great to get another big effort done.

It was not long before I was joining forces with Robert again to run the Allendale Challenge. We had to navigate ourselves up hills, across so many bogs and over lots of peat hags. It was tough, but it felt fantastic to finish and get my third marathon distance of the year done. I should mention at this point, that in my elevated mood, I had signed up for my first ever triathlon. The race was called 'The Lakesman' and it was ironman distance (of course). That equates to a 2.4 miles (3.9 kilometres) swim, followed by a 122 miles (180.2 kilometres) bike ride and finishing with 26.2 miles (42 kilometres) run. What could possibly go wrong? In all seriousness, this was a huge red flag of things to come, but it all seemed normal to me, despite the spending spree that ensued.

At the end of April, I returned to Stratford-upon Avon to run the Stratford Rotary Shakespeare Marathon, this is still my favourite road marathon. I had a great run and finished with a new personal best of 4.38.25, knocking eighteen minutes of my previous years' time. Although this would be a slow marathon time for many, I was (and still am) super proud of this time.

It was Early May and I was running in the tough enough Keswick Half Marathon again. This went well for me, again I succeeded in running the full route including the big climbs. This meant that with a time of 2.00.11, I had not only run this race over thirteen minutes quicker than the previous year, but I'd also knocked ten minutes of my personal best for my half marathon distance. It was shaping up to be a positive year of running for me.

My fifth marathon distance of 2015 was a return to the particularly challenging Mountain Trail26 Howgills Marathon. This was always going to be a tough ask, especially as I was full of cold. I was also having some painful symptoms of plantar fasciitis, signifying that the wheels were beginning to fall off. Despite this, I managed to get across the finish line in 07.20.47. Not brilliant, but at least I was now a quarter of the way to my target of 20 marathons.

Around three weeks later I was running in the Carlisle Tri Club 10k. This was a familiar route for me, and I was looking forward to it. The race went well, and I achieved another personal best. I had run the race in 49.37. I was ecstatic that I had finally ran sub-50 over the 10k distance. At the time this was a faster time than Kath had achieved over the distance, she did run eleven seconds quicker than my time at the Moorclose 10k the following year! It was nice to have bragging rights for a little while!

Things started to go a little wrong from here on. I continued doing a mixture of fell running and road running with Kath and Sam and although I was still getting some heel pain, I was really enjoying things. Unfortunately, the day after we ran up and down Helvellyn and a few days before I was scheduled to run the Ultimate Trails 110k, I had to see a doctor about my heel and leg. My heel was getting unbearably painful, and I'd found a lump on my right lower leg. The doctor prescribed me some strong anti-inflammatories to get me through the ultra on that weekend, but I was in too much pain, so I had to make the decision not to run. That was my first DNS (did not start).

I was later referred to the hospital for an x-ray and was found to have sustained a nasty stress fracture. This was terrible news for my running and triathlon challenges, and I had to withdraw from the lakesman triathlon and pretty much all my planned marathons and ultra marathons. I was absolutely gutted! With my right leg in an orthotic boot for at least eight weeks, the only exercise I was permitted to do was swimming.

I hate swimming, but I was in the local pool most days, trying to retain my fitness. I also tried my hand at open water swimming in Bassenthwaite Lake and Derwentwater with some friends and although it was a fantastic experience, I really lacked the confidence to test myself in the deeper water. After about eight weeks I could remove the boot and add in some cycling to my exercise regime. It wasn't until late September until I was given the all clear from my consultant to gradually start running again.

This was quite a challenging period for me mentally, but I was able to keep my mood at a manageable state most of the time. I built my mileage up relatively gradually and then ran in my first event back from injury. This was the Lakeland Trails Helvellyn Trail Challenge, a new race for me. It was fantastic being back pushing myself on the trails again. The route was stunning, and I really enjoyed the race. For me, time is not particularly relevant on that

153

type of terrain, but I was still quite pleased to run the fourteen-kilometre route in 1.38.45 in my first race back. About a week later, I ran in the Border Harrier Brampton to Carlisle road race. This was my longest run since May, and it felt like it too!

With reasonable regularity a local outdoor gear shop named George Fisher ran group trail runs to give runners an opportunity to test out Salomon trail and fell shoes, and sometimes Petzl head torches. The runs were usually led by fell and trail running legend, Ricky Lightfoot. Ricky was a Salomon sponsored athlete who has not only won many of the fell race classics, but he had also won a bunch of international races such as the Zegama-Aizkorri race in Spain, the Hammer Trail ultra marathon in Denmark, the Trail du Colorado in Réunion, the Dodo Trail in Mauritius and the Ultra Sky Marathon in Madeira. He also won the IAU (international association of ultra runners) Trail World Championships in 2013. So, he is not too bad at this running thing! Ricky was great at leading the George Fisher group runs, he is very humble and personable and always gives great advice. I ran on quite a few of these runs and always enjoyed them.

The Salomon trail running team would meet up for a training week in various parts of the world. As luck would have it, one of these training weeks was being held in the Cumbrian Lake District. Through George Fisher and Theatre by the Lake in Keswick there was opportunity to see some talks by some of the athletes, followed by a meet and greet and of course a group run. The opportunity to run with and chat with such elite athletes as Ricky Lightfoot, Emily Forseberg, Ryan Sandes, Mira Rai, Ellie Greenwood, Anna Frost, Ricky Gates and of course the male trail running GOAT (greatest of all time), Kilian Jornet. I've never been a prescriber of 'hero worshipping' of any kind and I still am not, however this was a fantastic opportunity to learn from the experts. Also, as it turns out, every one of them were genuine, humble, and down to earth human beings.

My first three marathon medals of 2014

A summit selfie with Kath

Setting off on day two of Hadrian's Wall

My three girls, keeping things real!

Me giving it the 'mountain-leg' on Causey Pike

Thea and Kilian Jornet after his incredible Bob Graham Round

Act Seven
Mania

Looking back to 2014 and my big year of marathons. I can admit that one marathon was clearly enough, however this made absolutely no sense to me at all at the time. Those fourteen marathons were unambiguous evidence that my rationality had been compromised. The fact that I had committed myself to running fourteen marathons should have terrified me, but it did not. I was just so excited with my challenge and not even the fear of failure entered my mind. My mood stayed elevated beyond the first two thirds of the project which helped me achieve things, though the final third was exceedingly difficult indeed. Using these marathons and ultra marathons to raise funds and awareness for Operation Turtle Dove was a straightforward thought process. I am not sure where my inspiration came from to link my cause to the sad extinction of the Passenger Pigeon, but I do believe it gave my message more power.

Along a similar vein to my Martha project, was my 'giving my right arm for Turkish wildlife' fundraising initiative. Prior to starting this project, I had never seriously contemplated, getting a tattoo. Travelling can send my mood into an elevated state and this was certainly the case when I returned from Türkiye. This time I knew the cause I was going to raise funds for, I just didn't know the how! In a very short space of time, I went from never seriously wanting to have a tattoo, to telling the world that I was going to get my arm tattooed for Turkish wildlife. I had written blog posts; I had been interviewed by television and newspaper journalists and booked my first tattoo session all before I had mentioned any of this to Kathleen. Knowing that she did not like tattoos may have been a reason subconsciously, but I just never thought to discuss this with her. I think I may have been of the idea that it was my body, so it was nobody else business what I did to it. The reality was that I was so focused on this project that nothing and nobody else seemed to matter. As with most of my manic episodes, this one came with a hefty price tag. I estimate that I spent in excess over £3,000.00, just on tattoos.

Once the tattoos started, I covered not just my right and left arms, but both and my hands and fingers, a sizeable portion of both legs, both sides of my neck, some of my chest and the right side of my head. That escalated very quickly! During all this, my mania was prominent, I do not know if there is any scientific research to back this up; but it is likely that the adrenaline or dopamine boost triggered by being tattooed, functioned as a stimulus for my mania.

During one of my manic episodes some years ago, I got fixated on pet reptiles and started researching what was available in the UK. I had never wanted a pet reptile before, mainly because, I did not feel ethically comfortable sacrificing live insects to keep the animals alive. However, with my mood as elevated as it was, all rationality and considerations were irrelevant anyway and the spending spree had begun. I ended up purchasing one Veiled Chameleon, two Panther Chameleon's, a Jackson's Chameleon, a Bearded Dragon, a Crested Gecko, a Packman Frog, two White's Tree Frogs and neither reptile nor amphibian, a pair of Madagascan Giant Hissing Cockroaches, I mean, why not, right? This haul of new pets may not seem too excessive, a little unusual perhaps, but was it worthy of identification as manic behaviour? So far, the expenditure was around the £560.00 mark, certainly more than we could afford raising a family on one reasonably low wage. Things were about to get worse as now I had purchased the menagerie, I needed to buy the housing and all the paraphernalia needed to keep the animals happy and healthy. I bought two huge cabinets to house the chameleons, five smaller cabinets for the remaining creatures, six heating systems and basking spots, five UV/UVB lights as well as bowls, feeder insects etc. This put the spend up to around £1,600.00. For context, this was more than Kath was bringing home in pay each month. This was not good, and it wasn't acceptable.

There have been quite a few incidents of manic episodes triggering serious overspending since early adulthood, these and risky behaviours I have engaged in always leave me with deep guilt and regret once my elevated mood drops. I am a caring, empathetic, and considerate person (at least I hope I am), so when I look back at my manic behaviours, it hurts. I realise I have become apparently selfish, single-minded, and lacking any empathy or consideration, and it breaks my heart.

Although my behaviours whilst in an elevated mood can be perceived as selfish, I see this differently. I consider being selfish as a conscious choice, whereas when I am manic my rationality and decision making is usually very impaired. I usually believe that whatever behaviour I am engaged in is part of a greater plan or vitally important for everyone. Delusions of grandeur? One important thing I have had embrace is that I am solely responsible for my actions, and I cannot and should not use the fact that I have bipolar as an excuse or free pass for unacceptable behaviour. If I allowed myself to use bipolar as an excuse for every negative or stupid behaviour I do, this would inhibit my attempts to manage my condition. Ultimately, the buck stops with me!

Mania has not always been a negative impact of my life; I have also had some amazing life experiences due to my elevated mood. There is a lengthy list of creative geniuses that have been diagnosed with (or are largely considered to have) bipolar disorder. These

160

include Vincent van Gogh, Francis Ford Coppola, Richard Dreyfuss, Carrie Fisher, Stephen Fry, Edvard Munch, Kanye West, Isaac Newton and possibly Kurt Cobain. A fine list of some very talented and groundbreaking creative thinkers and doers. I should state here that considering I possess no real skills or talent, the only thing I have in common with these people is that I have a diagnosis of bipolar. A creative genius I am not! That may sound self-deprecating, but the facts are what they are. I might not be a creative genius, but I can, particularly when I am manic, have some interesting creative ideas.

My '1000 miles in memory of Martha' fundraising project, was one such idea. With the expense of race entries, travel, and my talk tour aside, this project overall was a very positive experience, certainly earlier on in the process at least. For someone who had only just started running a few months previously to choose to enter the ballot for the London Marathon could be considered relatively abnormal behaviour. Having forgotten I'd even applied for this marathon place; it was a surprise when my place was confirmed. Most people with normal neurology would have been a little nervous about the prospect of running London Marathon and either withdrawn their entry or started training, focusing on that single challenging event. I would like to think that I would make those same more sensible choices if my mental state was balanced.

Although mania does make me feel incredible when at its peak, with feelings of elation, indestructibility, and importance, it is the part of my condition that I fear and dread the most. Feeling energised and needing little sleep for an extended period is exhausting and really cannot be sustainable. The biggest fear I have from mania is losing control of my mind, particularly my decision making. The behaviours born out of this can be very destructive and frequently expensive. Not having full control of my rationality is a very scary reality. There has been some scientific research that suggests overtime manic or depressive episodes do cause changes in the grey matter in the brain, the frontal lobes in particular. In recent times, I am convinced I notice changes in my personality and decision making, especially following a manic episode. This is a personal concern for the future.

The National Health Service (NHS) community mental health team where I am based is overall, quite good. It certainly isn't perfect and there are areas that need improvement to help protect the health of more venerable people. Because of my mental health condition, I need consistency, structure, and stability, without this, things can unravel very quickly. Within the first nine months of my diagnosis, I had seen four different psychiatrists. This was exhausting, as I had to go through the same probing and uncomfortable questions about my life with each doctor.

Thankfully in recent years there has been more consistency and I have seen the same psychiatrist for several years now. When it comes to care coordinators and community mental health nurses (CPN's), my experience is similar, but slightly better. I have had at least four different CPN's or care coordinators since my diagnosis, which has made it difficult to build up a good trust, which really is important. Whilst I have never met a CPN I did not like, I did not feel like I could fully trust any of them, apart from one. I did not feel like most of them had my best interests at heart, they seemed to be more interested in discharging me back to my GP than listening to me and facilitating the care I needed. This is a frustrating, particularly when you are trying to understand your condition and how you can best manage it. This coupled with feeling like you are being experimented on because of the enormous range of medication combinations you have had to try, can really set back any potential recovery.

This might be more a reflection on me, rather than the service, but I felt like I was treated like a child rather than an adult. For example, on one occasion I missed a physical health check up with the community mental health team because I was extremely ill at the time. There is high potential that physical damage caused by mental health medications and conditions that bipolar can predispose a person to have, physical health checks should be conducted with reasonable regularity. Unfortunately, due to me missing one appointment because of my condition, it was over two years before I was offered another appointment for this. It is like they did not care, and it certainly reinforced my feeling that they had no practical understanding of my illness.

I learnt not to trust the service or at least accepted that they could only serve a basic function for me. If I was going manage this disorder, I was going to have to do the bulk of the heavy lifting. Following diagnosis, I was under the assumption that the medication available to me would in effect 'cure' me of my symptoms. Unfortunately, this was wishful thinking, because it seems, life is never that simple. In my experience bipolar medication has the effect that can be compared to taking a paracetamol for a migraine, they can take the edge off, just enough for you to cope a little better.

My relationship with my diagnosis has changed a lot over the years. Initially I completely accepted it and believed that this was key to me managing the condition. In this context, I thought that language was important, and I would describe myself as bipolar, I was owning the diagnosis. This seemed to work for a while, but the deeper I involved myself into the bipolar communities, the more I realised I was becoming the illness. The next stage was really a mix of acceptance and denial. The acceptance part was really focused on my compliance with taking my prescribed medication, I've never purposefully missed a dose. However, the rest of my position was denial. I removed myself from all bipolar related websites and forums and changed my narrative from 'I am bipolar' to 'I have bipolar.' I tried to separate the condition from me as a person. This made so much sense to me at the time as it made me feel more in control of my situation. I still had some doubt about my diagnosis at that time, so I thought this new perception helped me keep the bipolar tag at arm's length. This seemed to work well for many years, until I noticed a deterioration in my symptoms. Things came to a head when I had a series of severe manic episodes followed by the expected depression. This really changed me; it was impossible to separate the bipolar from me. This was already the point of no return, I knew that there was now no question that my bipolar diagnosis was correct, this had only taken seven years!

Whilst all this was going on with my mental health, my birding activities were continuing to dwindle. My last twitches were to see Ring-necked Duck and American Green-winged Teal in Dumfries and Galloway and a fantastic Citrine Wagtail at Longtown, found by my friend Chris. My last bird photograph I took, was of a Glaucous Gull in Whitehaven Harbour. Having spent over thirty-eight years with birding and twitching in my life, I never thought I would be without it. I had been so lucky to see so many interesting and beautiful birds, see some amazing places and most of all, meet a bunch of amazing and varied people. However, my interest in pursuing this had been waning for some time, due mostly to the deterioration of my mental health.

It pains me to say this, as I know it would not be what he had wanted for me; but when my dear friend Martin Garner died, I lost my motivation and ambition to continue doing anything related to birds or birding. I sold my binoculars and my telescope on a whim, something I still momentarily regret on occasion. I did continue to go out locally with Chris and Peter (Chris had spare optics that he was kind enough to let me use), and whilst it was nice to catch up with my friends, it became increasingly apparent that I had lost interest in birding completely. I still miss the excitement I used to get from seeing a rare bird or facing a tricky identification challenge and of course the human social side of it all, but my already complicated mind is a little less strained without it.

During the following few years, I continued with my running and cycling, but I think my new obsession with the gym had overtaken my wildlife interest. Don't get me wrong, I still enjoyed wildlife, you can't shake a lifelong interest just like that, but I was spending a lot less time studying it. At the gym I was continuing to go to spinning classes and adding in several other classes. At the peak of it, I was at the gym every day for four hours or so. I was not getting any fitter or slimmer!

Because of my excessive weight gain I was referred to Slimming World for help. I really did not enjoy the evangelical environmental there, but I stuck it out for the three months I'd committed to. I managed to shed around a stone (6.4 kilos) in weight, but I put it back on (and some) very soon afterwards. After this I was referred to my local NHS cottage hospital to the physiotherapy department. They ran a group that focused on weight loss through exercise. It was a pleasant group to attend, the NHS staff were very good, knowledgeable, supportive, and caring. I made some nice friends among the attendees too. The course was made up of two main topics, food, and exercise. The food and nutrition talks were useful as a refresher, but they really did not tell me anything I didn't already know. My issue was not a lack of knowledge about what and how much I should eat but trying to put that into action. The exercise element was quite basic, but I enjoyed participating. Exercise was something I had very well covered. I did get the impression that the National Health Service was not set up to help with the source of my bipolar health problems, but merely apply the metaphorical plasters where needed. I realised early on that the only person that could help with my physical problems was me. The main issue here was that I was quite unreliable!

I continued erratically to try tackle my weight gain and hide away as much as I could from my mental illness using excessive exercise. I could see however that things were continuing a downward spiral. This was not the best of times!

In 2017 I was still running regularly, but due to declining fitness, I was getting much slower and finding it a lot more challenging. In February I ran in the iconic Carnethy 5 Hill Race on the Pentlands for my fourth and last time. The extreme winter weather conditions meant that for the first time a cut-off time before the final climb of the race was implemented, this didn't bode well for me. The high winds, thick snow and compacted ice made an already tough course into a significantly more challenging race. It was a proper adventure and I really enjoyed it. Disappointedly, I missed the cut-off by around 30 seconds. This meant I had to run the still challenging trail back to the start. Not the ending I wanted, but it was completely understandable given the conditions. Although I did not know it at the time, but this was a sign of things to come. The next event I ran in was the Trail26 Dalmain 10k. My pace had well and truly left me, but I did get around what was a challenging cross-country-esque course. I found it tough going, but it was nice to finish a race for once!

Outside of races, I was running regularly with Kath, Sam, and a few other friends as well as my local running club. My times were getting slower which was something I was having to accept. Ignoring this frustration, I was still enjoying my running, particularly on trail and fell. My next event was the D20, a 20-mile race that was part of the Dale Trail Series. The race started in the village of Reeth on the northern part of the Yorkshire Dales. The weather conditions were quite warm to start and then thunderstorms and localised flooding thrown in for good measure. Electric storms are not the best idea when you are at the top of a big climb! Unfortunately, my pace was letting me down again, as I was timed out at around eight miles into the race. Another disappointing DNF, but I had at least given it my best on that day.

Barefoot running is best described as either running with no shoes or running with shoes designed to simulate bare feet. I bought a pair of these barefoot shoes, they had no support or cushioning, and their main function was to protect my soles from abrasion and punctures. I had hoped that using these shoes would strengthen up my feet and hopefully cure the plantar fasciitis that had been a problem for some time. I followed advice and built up my running time in them gradually. Unfortunately, they didn't really work for me, they seemed to exasperate the leg and foot problems I'd had since childhood, so back to my plushily cushioned Hoka's it was!

In August I was on the south and southwest coasts of England visiting family and participating in the Mudcrew Events RED RAT trail race. The route started in Porthloe near St Austell in Cornwall and followed the beautiful coastal path eastwards for twenty miles. This was my main race of the year, so I set off with some anticipation. However, not with all the anticipation in the world could drag me twenty miles given my declining fitness. I stopped just at the eight-and-a-half mile mark at Gorran Haven. Disappointed of course, but also happy to finish running. My DNF collection was getting uncomfortably large.

During 2018 I continued with my gym obsession and did not participate in any running events at all. My fitness continued to free fall, and my confidence was shot to pieces. In fact, I did no consistent running until June. I did run more consistently after then, mostly with Kath or Sam on local trails, fells, and road. This was an unbelievably bad sign of things to come.

On a more positive note, I started longboarding with Sam, I was rubbish at it, but it was still really good fun! Fairly random I know, but why not!

The following year I was trying to get more consistent with my running, in the hope I would start to see some improvements. I continued running shorter distances on the trails and fells, as well as a little on the road. I was still struggling a bit, but still enjoying getting in amongst the countryside.

One morning, I woke up in the night with quite severe abdominal pains. I thought this was something I needed to get checked out by a doctor. This was in the days when you could easily get a face-to-face appointment with your GP! After an examination, my doctor sent me to hospital with a suspected appendicitis. Following a CT scan and some blood tests, I was told I did not have appendicitis and was sent home with some co-codamol to help with the pain. This was certainly a relief as I did not really like the idea of a stay in hospital. I went about my business as usual, thankfully the medication helped with the pain. I spent an afternoon helping Sam lay concrete down for his home improvements.

The following night the pain came back with vengeance. It was so bad I was unable to sleep. I didn't think it was appendicitis having already received the all clear from hospital for that. I thought perhaps that I'd strained some muscles with the bit of manual work I'd done a day or so previously. As the day progressed, I was feeling very unwell and I had been physically sick.

Now, my youngest daughter Thea was at home with me as she had caught a sickness bug. I assumed this was what I was suffering with. As we got into early-evening, the pain had got significantly worse, and I really didn't know what to do. I thought I would maybe wait until the morning and then call my doctor, however the intensity of the pain, changed my mind and I called Cumbria Health on Call (CHoC), the local out of hours medics.

I was sent to the CHoC surgery in Wigton and examined as well as the usual blood pressure, blood oxygen and body temperature measured. The doctor informed me that he had called an ambulance as he was sure that I had sepsis, probably caused by cholecystitis. I was not expecting this, I felt very unwell, but I didn't think I'd be rushed to hospital in an emergency! I knew that sepsis could be fatal, but I really was not worried, I didn't feel like I was likely to die. Besides, by this stage in my life, having lived with

168

bipolar symptoms for longer than I would like, death did not scare me at all, dying perhaps, but not death.

After some great care by the paramedics, I was seen virtually instantly on arrival to accident and emergency, by one of the doctors. I remember the doctor telling me I was extremely sick, but I would be okay now. They hooked me up to one of many antibiotic solutions and gave me morphine and liquid paracetamol for pain relief. The first twenty-four hours I was on a bed in the corridor of A&E, spanning my birthday of all days! I was eventually admitted into the hospital and placed in a ward. My bed was in a private room initially, which I much preferred.

However, during my stay I was moved to three or four busy rooms where my social anxiety was tested to its uncomfortable limit. I do not know why it took more than three days for me to get an ultrasound on my abdomen, particularly as I had to fast the whole time prior, but I was glad to get it done. The scan confirmed what the doctors had suspected, acute cholecystitis, infected gallbladder (caused by a large build-up of stones). I was feeling very unwell still, I was hallucinating and strangely waking myself up shouting. The surgeon came to see me to discuss surgery options and then it was just a waiting game for a bed to be free in the operating theatre.

I do not know if it was solely due to my physical illness or perhaps because of the difficult social side of being kept in hospital, but my mood had dropped into a fairly bad depressed state. Occupying my mind became a challenging task, I could not find any useful distractions as my concentration was very short. The only break I felt was good, was when Kathleen, Shannon, Erin and Thea came to see me during the far too short vising time. I was also quite anxious about my impending operation. I had read about people being operated on when the paralysed part of the anaesthetic worked, but the memory blocker and pain free part failed. It sounded horrible and something I was terrified that I would experience.

169

I was told that I would probably have the operation later that day. The surgeon explained most of the details and I signed the consent form and waited. Unfortunately, the operating theatre was too busy for me, but the operation was given the go ahead the following day. That morning, I had a visit from the anaesthesiologist who informed me of an additional complication to my operation. Usually when people are intubated prior to their surgery, they are anesthetized first. Unfortunately, because I have severe obstructive sleep apnoea, I would have to have a camera inserted into my respiratory tract to guide the tube into the correct place before I would be anesthetized. This sounded awful and certainly added more fuel to my pre surgery anxiety. When I went into theatre the anaesthesiologist explained once again what was going to happen. He told me to tap my finger if the process was too much for me and he would stop and go with plan b, I never knew what plan b was of course! After inserting another cannula into the back of one of my hands, I got to choose the genre of music playing in the theatre.

I chose wisely, I chose metal! Next a light anaesthetic was sprayed into my throat as the camera was inserted. This was a very unpleasant experience to be honest, but I held out until I felt like I was being asphyxiated and tapped my finger to let the doctor know that I had reached my limit. He said very calmly that it was okay, and it was all done. The very next thing I was aware of was waking up in the recovery area after my operation. My legs were strapped into inflatable compression boots, and I was in very imminent need of a bladder voiding. The nurse looking after me, gave me a receptacle to urinate into, but I was unable to perform, stage fright and all that. Once I was returned to the ward, I was temporarily released from the leg compression system and with great relief I was able to void my bladder. The compression paraphernalia was used to reduce the occurrence of blood clots post-operation. I knew the operation didn't go exactly smoothly

170

because I had a drain hanging out one of my abdominal holes! This was a concern.

After a reasonable night's sleep, I was feeling a lot better physically with a lot less pain. The surgeon came around to check up on me and tell me how the operation went.

Although the operation was conducted using laparoscopy (keyhole surgery), I had to be opened up a bit more than planned, due to the difficulty of my particular case. My gallbladder was a bit of a mess as the infection had been quite severe causing it to be ruptured into an almost unrecognisable state. It was fused to part of my abdomen that it had no business attaching itself to. Suffice to say, it was a more complicated surgery than was expected, hence the drain.

Despite all that, the surgeon was happy with the outcome. I was pleased the operation had gone well, but my mental health was really struggling. The few coping strategies that I had were failing and I was in a bad way. About eight days into my in-patient stay and I was finally told I was going to be discharged. They removed my cannula and the drain (that was a bit stingy, but not as bad as I was expecting) and I asked Kath to come and collect me. I was all set and excited! Things rarely follow a straight line, and just I was almost out the door, I was told that my blood test showed that I still had quite a bad infection, so I had to stay in the hospital for a bit longer. This was disappointing, though there was not much I could do about it. Thankfully, I was given the all clear and sent home the following day. It was so good to be home with my family again.

That was my first stay in hospital as a patient. The nursing staff, doctors, surgeons etc, were fantastically professional, approachable, and caring in relation to my physical health. The important thing that was missing, was mental health care. Given that they were aware of my psychiatric illness, you would expect some level of mental health care. This was sadly lacking during my stay.

Once I was at home, I had to avoid heavy lifting and exercise (except walking) for a month or so, but I was back running again by mid-June. I was still finding it difficult, but it did feel great to be back at it again. We have a local nature reserve locally called Watchtree. This former airfield had a bit of a sad start to it being a wildlife reserve, the site was used for burying or incinerating the colossal number of sheep and cattle killed because of the badly handled foot and mouth disease disaster. I can think of no better use of that land than a nature reserve.

The reserve has developed into a beautiful patchwork of pools, wildflower meadows and woodland. What's more it is a safe environment for wheelchair users, walkers, cyclists and runners, everyone, whatever their ability. They hold a broad range of events to raise funds for their charity. There was one in September 2019 that particularly caught my attention.

It was the 100mph 24-hour challenge. The idea was for wheelchair users, runners and walkers to complete as many laps as possible around the reserve circumference (two miles, approximately) within the 24 hours. Participants could complete as many laps as the wanted. The goal was for the accumulative total to give the average of one hundred miles completed per hour. I liked the idea of this challenge, no time pressures, I could just see what I could do on that given day. My plan was to keep going for the full 24 hours, but knowing how poor my fitness was, I decided to walk it all. I really enjoyed the event, the format really worked well. I succeeded in continuing for the full twenty-four hours and managed to walk forty-four miles in total, my furthest continuous distance covered. This felt good!

Since my hospital stay, my mood had continued to plummet, to the extent that I was struggling to cope with daily life. To be brutally honest, I just did not want to live anymore, life was a continuous struggle and even when things were seemingly balanced, there was no quality. I had even started researching the easiest ways to die, there is no such thing by the way. The closest I came to dying by suicide was when I stood on the fourth rail of the footbridge that crosses the Wigton bypass. I do not know if it was natural fear that stopped me, or concern that my actions could cause the death of a driver that stopped me. I would like to think it was the latter.

Things were very bad; this prompted my care coordinator to fast track an appointment for me with a psychiatrist. True to form, it was yet another psychiatrist I had not previously seen. This meant going over everything again. It seemed a harder ask this time. The psychiatrist agreed with my previous diagnosis, but with the specification of Bipolar 2 with severe depression. He also agreed that the medication I was taking, was not working well enough, so suggested we tried a drug called Lithium. Lithium is quite an old medication, but it is still considered the gold standard for treating bipolar symptoms.

Given these facts, I am not sure why my previous psychiatrists had not opted for this in the first place. This psychiatrist explained to me that once I started taking lithium, I would have to make sure I drank at least two and a half litres of water every day as dehydration can cause very serious problems. I was given a booklet and a card that I was told to carry with me. Lithium is quite a complicated medication, the doctor cannot simply prescribe you a therapeutic dose based on your weight or age, because it's all about the moles, or should I say mmols! I'm not exactly sure what a mole or millimole is, but it has something to do with atoms, molecules and free radicals.

If I understand it correctly a mmol is an SI unit used to show the mass of a substance that is identified in a solution. So, in the case of lithium, I was started on a low dose and had weekly blood tests to find the mmols of lithium in a litre of my blood. The dosage was

173

increased until the amount of lithium in my body was at a therapeutic level, this is generally considered to be between 0.4 and 1.0 mmol/l. My levels settled at 0.8 mmol/l, which equated to lithium dosage of 1200 mg/day.

Despite my tattoos, I've had a fear of needles since childhood, but I had to get used to having blood tests regularly. The weekly blood monitoring continued until my levels had stabilised and then the monitoring was monthly for some time and now my blood is monitored every three months. I did get used to blood tests, they are no big deal to me now, injections on the other hand, well, I'm still not keen! In addition to the lithium, I was prescribed the atypical antipsychotic aripiprazole. These two medications together began to improve my mental state slightly, though I was still trapped in a depressive episode. The manic episodes stayed dormant. This seemed like a positive situation at the time. I was certainly struggling, but there was still some noticeable improvement.

As with many psychiatric medications, lithium would take a few months at a therapeutic level before it really became noticeably beneficial. There are no quick fixes with mental illness unfortunately. I had no choice, but to be patient. As time progresses, my depression, although still in present, was significantly lighter. I was beginning to feel a little bit more positive about my life. That glimmer of possibilities, for me, was huge.

Heading into 2020, I was still hiding from my diagnosis as much as I could, although I was still fully compliant with my medication. When I had won in the mental illness lottery with bipolar, little did I know I'd won double bubble! Although the actual number varies from study to study, the average indicates that people who have bipolar will have a life expectancy eight to twenty years shorter than healthy people without bipolar. If you have bipolar and are reading this, do not worry, knowing what the risk factors are gives you the power to make sure you reduce them or remove them altogether.

Mental illness is always separated from physical illness, it really shouldn't be.

The way I see it is that at the very least mental illness affects the brain and the brain is a physical part of the body. Therefore, mental illness should at the very least be treated under the same umbrella as physical illness. Mental illness is treated secondary to physical illness, putting people's lives at serious risk on a regular basis. For example, some patients are having to wait months and months to get their first appointment. Once you are in the system it is a frequent occurrence to have your appointments cancelled at the last minute, with a replacement appointment not sent out until many weeks or sometimes months later.

I personally need to have my time and plans firmly structured, otherwise I can become unwell. I get quite concerned and anxious preceding an appointment with the community mental health team, when they are cancelled at short notice this can have quite a serious negative impact on my mental health and leave me feeling inferior and unimportant. I understand why the appointments may need to be cancelled, the service is stretched due to insufficient funding and high staff turnover rate. This really needs to change; I don't think I'm being overdramatic in saying that people are dying as a result of this situation. Why physical illness is prioritized over mental illness I really do not understand. Fighting to get vital support is exhausting and for someone with bipolar or other psychiatric illnesses there is a limit to how much energy you have available.

At the beginning of 2020, my fitness had continued to deteriorate, and my weight was worryingly still increasing. I was still trying to run, but it was getting frustratingly difficult. As January was ending, I was getting a very worrying symptom. This was a tight discomfort in my chest that radiated along to my left shoulder. I had a good idea, what this was, so I went to see my doctor. My doctor was quite concerned and prescribed a glyceryl trinitrate (GTN) spray and a daily dose of aspirin. She also referred me to the hospital for an echocardiogram.

Things escalated quite quickly when my ECG showed some sort of anomaly that warranted further investigation. Next, I was given an appointment for an angiogram. This, I was not looking forward to, in fact I was terrified. My health issues were starting to feel serious. I was quite concerned about what might be found through the investigations and of course I was very anxious about the procedure. The day of my appointment arrived, and I was asked to arrive around 8am if I remember correctly.

The procedure was explained to me, and I was asked if I wanted mild sedation. Of course, I wanted sedation, they were going to shove a cannula into my radial artery and up towards my heart! There were a few emergencies into the lab before me, but after several hours of nervousness, it was my turn. Laying down on the bed in the laboratory, I was quite surprised by the number of medical staff needed for the procedure. I was given some mild sedation and a local anaesthetic into my right wrist. The cannula was then forced into my radial artery, it took a couple of attempts to get it right. It is a bit of a weird sensation, feeling something alien moving about in your vascular system whilst there is lots of discussion in technical language relating to navigation and findings. The chief doctor told me that they had not found any arterial blockages, but they had found some furring inside some of my arteries. He gave me the diagnosis of angina pectoris and requested that my GP prescribed a daily dose of a beta blocker for me.

After the procedure, a plastic contraption was compressed onto my wrist and I had to wait in the recovery area for around four hours, just to be certain I wasn't going to bleed everywhere! A few weeks later I had an ultrasound of my heart to check that there were no further problems with my cardiovascular system. My heart was fine, which came as a huge relief of course. Unfortunately, I was told that I couldn't run anymore, and it was very unlikely that I would ever be able to run again (I liked those odds, it sounded like a challenge to me)! In all seriousness, I was disappointed with this news, although I was quietly relieved because running had become so frustratingly difficult.

My angina symptoms had got quite a bit worse; I was getting an attack by just going up the stairs in my home. I don't really know if the GTN spray was working or if the symptoms eased off because I had stopped moving. My GP phoned me up to check how my symptoms were, when I told her about a recent angina episode that had lasted over four hours, she told me off. I should have phoned for an ambulance immediately. I survived though!

My doctor increased my beta blocker dose and added in a couple more medications including a calcium channel blocker. I was beginning to rattle! I think my angina diagnosis must have triggered a series of appointments in various hospital departments. For example, I was seen by a doctor in relation to my blood pressure and kidneys. I had to wear a blood pressure monitor for twenty-four hours, lots more blood tests and fill a big receptacle with my special brand of urine for 24 hours. I was living life, that was for sure! I did have hypertension and was prescribed medication for this, and thankfully my kidneys were fine. I was put well and truly on the scary bus again, when the consultant examined my abdomen and noticed that I had one inverted nipple. He was concerned enough to invite his colleague across who was a cancer specialist.

After a quick examination, he referred me for further investigation. Not what I was expecting and not what I wanted. A week or so later I was back to hospital and sitting in the very pink waiting room of the breast screening clinic. I felt very out of place, which was not improved by the confused glances I got from some of the women waiting for their consultations. It turns out men can get breast cancer, who knew! After my breast scan, I was very relieved to be told that there were no signs of cancer in my man boobs. That was the best news I'd had for a while.

The next major health issue to surface was the global covid19 pandemic. We had seen this building after the first cases came to light in China. I certainly did not expect this disease to spread across the world so quickly. When it hit the UK, the reality really was unavoidable. People were dying of this virus in substantial numbers. Our government was more focussed on filling their pockets off the pandemic scraps rather than managing the crisis to reduce the fatalities. When the first lockdown started, it felt like we were in the middle of a social experiment. It was weirdly exciting at first, not being able to mix with people was not a major issue for me. I had been practicing that skill for years. Another bonus was having my kids at home, the entertainment with those three seemed infinite!

Online shopping was far too easy, so I ordered a stupid amount of stuff I did not need or want, although the bulk buy of Cadbury's crème eggs went down well with all the family! Most days we were brought crashing down to reality with the daily death toll report. This was always very sobering, particularly as I was categorised as high risk. Despite the lockdown rules it was still necessary for me to keep on schedule with my blood monitoring. There was lots of biosecurity in place of course. On one of my surgery visits I was hit with the unwelcome double whammy of the diagnoses of diabetes type-two and morbid obesity. I really was winning at life! The diabetes was initially managed with diet and medication then as the disease progressed a weekly self-administered injection was added to the therapy. Those injections terrified me at first, but they were not as bad as my brain was telling me they would be. As for the morbid obesity, well that was a work in progress. People who have a diagnosis of bipolar can be predisposed to suffer from cardiovascular disease, diabetes type-two and obesity. I had dealt the cards and got a full house! This was now a serious situation and if I didn't do something to reverse the progression, I would be dead before my time. You would think for someone who regularly flirts with suicide, I would welcome this fast-track to the black. It turns

178

out that I am either a coward or a control freak, either way, when I go, it will be on my own terms.

Sam would drop by regularly during lockdown to check on me. Initially a quick chat through the window and then once restrictions were relaxed a little, we would get out for a walk, socially distanced of course. These visits were important for me, particularly with what I was going through at the time.

During the first lockdown I found myself in an elevated mood, full of energy and excitement. I had not felt like this for a good while, but it felt good. I do not actually know what triggered this, given my deteriorating health, I really didn't have much to be energised about. There always seems to be an obsession that fuels my manic periods, and this episode was no different. I was fixated on creating a YouTube channel about local wildlife, predominantly invertebrates. I maxed out my credit card on a new phone capable of taking high quality video, some microphones and adapters, some lighting and backdrops, some gimbals, and some videography app subscriptions. Then whilst awaiting delivery of those items, I spent hours and hours watching videos teaching me the best practices to creating and managing a YouTube channel.

Once my equipment arrived and my channel was created, I began seeking out wildlife to film, initially along the bridleway near my home and then a little further afield once covid restrictions allowed. This was a very enjoyable period, finding interesting wildlife was always exciting and delving into the research side of things was fascinating. I uploaded a couple of videos a week, which kept me very busy. I started getting some nice feedback from people who had watched some of them, this gave me the little bit of confidence to continue with the channel. Although I was getting a growing number of subscribers, I never had enough to trigger any remuneration. I did manage to feature some interesting flora and fauna including Marsh Fritillary, White-faced Darter, Narrow-bordered Five-spot Burnet Moth, Small Skipper, Bird's-nest Orchid, Bog Orchid, and Early Marsh Orchid.

Another big positive element to this latest obsession was that my youngest daughter, Thea, was keen to get involved and help me find some interesting beasts. Thea got particularly interested in spiders and harvestmen, she certainly had no fear. We would go out around the village at night with torches and see how many different species of spiders we could find; it was more than you would think! Because one YouTube channel was not enough of a commitment and my manic component was at this point, driving the juggernaut, I set up around four other YouTube channels at the same time. A big shiny red flag, right there! My additional channels included one that focussed on my health (more of a vlog style) and another where I reacted to anti-atheist memes.

During this period of manic or hypomanic behaviour, I immersed myself in pro-atheism videos for days and days or more accurately weeks and weeks. This had become a textbook case of confirmation bias. It got to the point that I'd become evangelical about atheism, I'm sure you get the irony with that! I was exhibiting that bipolar staple of grandiose thinking. I thought that I could educate the world with my crappy little YouTube channel.

If you build it, they will come, they did not! When I am not in amongst an episode, I still fit the criteria of an agnostic atheist, but I do not shout about it. I respect people who believe in a god or gods if anything I am a little envious of their faith. I have met a fair number of Christians, practicing Jews, Muslims, Hindus, Sikhs, Jehovah's witnesses and Pagans over the years and most of them have been decent and caring individuals. I have no issue with people following any religion, providing they treat other people with consideration and love.

It is when religion is used as an excuse to kill, segregate, and persecute that I find impossible to stomach. I understand why humans are drawn to believing in the existence of a higher being, it gives them a reason for life and helps to take away the fear of mortality. It does give an answer to a lot of the existential questions. I think I have too many questions that can't seem to be answered.

My obsessive YouTube period ended, when I decided that it was taking too much of my time away from photographing and recording invertebrates along my local bridleway. I was spending four or five hours meticulously searching the vegetation along the track every day and then a further two or three hours trying to identify everything that I had managed to photograph. This was a lot, even for me! Sam visited me for one of my bridleway saunters on a couple of occasions, both times he asked me if I was manic. He was right of course, but I just could not see it, even when the possibility was brought to my attention. There are usually positive aspects about my manic periods. In this case it was spending more time with Thea and finding an ichneumon (a type of parasitic wasp) that was new to Cumbria. Something changes with me because of a manic episode, presumably sustained damage to my brain. In this instance I can no longer try to look at invertebrates without feeling physically sick. Weird, I know!

With the very worrying deterioration of my physical health during 2021, I was on a mission to stop the rot, the following year. After trying various weight loss programs, none of which worked for me in the long-term. I was at a loss what to do next. My doctor suggested that she could refer me to the bariatric clinic in Liverpool. This was quite a dramatic step to take, but nothing else was working and my life would likely be shortened if I couldn't start to reverse the curve.

At my first appointment they took my vital statistics and then told me what the process was. I had to attend a lot of in person appointments at Liverpool and quite a few telephone appointments. If I complied with all of this, then I would have the option of surgery, providing I was healthy enough for the operation. This was going to be a very long process, certainly no quick fix. I attended the first few sets of appointments, and everything was going in the right direction.

In the back end of June, we were experiencing a heatwave, and I became quite ill. I had sickness and diarrhoea and was really struggling to keep myself hydrated. Anything I ate or drank seemed to leave by the quickest route possible. After three weeks I had shed nearly three stone (19 kilos). I phoned the NHS 111 service and the doctor suggested I ate some kefir yoghurt! Things continued to get worse, and I suspected that it had something to do with the levels of lithium in my blood. I spoke to my GP and after I had my blood tested the results revealed that my lithium levels had spiked and were bordering on toxic levels.

I was promptly sent to A&E. As always it was quite a long wait, and given we were amidst a global pandemic, the situation was a little more stressful than usual. Once I was seen by one of the doctors, I had a blood test, which mirrored the one I had had at my doctor's surgery. The doctor sent me home with some anti-sickness tablets. The next day my blood was retested, and the lithium serum concentration was even higher, so I was sent back to accident and emergency again. This time I was instructed to reduce my lithium dose and then sent home. I was getting the feeling that they had not encountered someone with lithium toxicity very often. I was back at my GP surgery the following day for yet another blood test.

My doctor phoned me with my results, and she was quite concerned. The results showed that not only were my lithium levels extremely high, but my kidneys were showing signs of damage. My doctor insisted that I returned to A&E, she had phoned ahead, so the medical team were expecting me. This was getting exhausting, but I returned to the emergency department and after about four hours the medical team saw me, and I was finally admitted to a ward. One of the nurses looking after me, knowing my psychiatric condition, was quite concerned about me. She took the time to check up on me and alerted the crisis team to my case.

I do not know if the nurse thought this was a suicide attempt, which it wasn't, but it was nice to have someone looking out for me. When it comes to drawing blood for testing, well I'm was quite used to it by then. The problem I had, was that I only have one arm that is good for giving blood, and that arm already had a cannula in it. Because of the toxic levels of lithium in my blood, I was given a constant supply of a saline solution through a drip and having blood tests every hour for the first eight hours or so. The doctors found it quite a challenge taking blood from me, at one point they attempted twice in my hand and three times in my foot before they succeeded back in my arm. It was a lot of fun as I'm sure you can imagine!

Once the doctors were happy with my lithium levels, I only had to have my blood tested once a day. I was sent for a CT scan the following day. The gastrointestinal consultant visited me to tell me that the scans had shown some swelling in my colon. I was not surprised with this news as I hadn't been able to keep anything in my body for weeks! I would have been sent for an endoscopy appointment (and not via the throat...) once one became available. Well, that was something to look forward to (it really wasn't)! I was still feeling very unwell and couldn't eat anything, which was probably a bit of a self-fulfilling prophecy.

On a more positive note, as well as my lithium tablets, the doctor in charge had stopped all my diabetes medication as my blood glucose levels were far too low. This was fantastic news to me; I certainly wouldn't miss those injections. I was in hospital for five days, and during my stay my mental health took quite a severe downward dip. This was not surprising given the strain of my physical illness, the difficulty of being in the hospital environment and of course because I was no longer taking any mood stabilisers. I was visited by the crisis team, which was good to some extent. The hospital psychiatrist did ask me some quite pointed questions suggesting that he thought I may have purposefully taken an overdose of lithium. This was not the case, but I guess it's important for the mental health professionals to be certain. I was discharged from hospital a few days later and an appointment with my psychiatrist for the following day.

At my appointment we discussed what had happened to cause my lithium serum levels to get so dangerously high and what we needed to do next in relation to my bipolar medication. Given that I had previously tried a wide range of medications and the only one that seemed to help was lithium, I was keen to give it another try. My psychiatrist agreed with me and so we put a plan in place to introduce lithium again, very gradually. This meant going back to weekly blood tests until a safe therapeutic level had been achieved. One thing I had to get on top of was my hydration. Drinking a minimum of two and a half litres of water every day was essential to safeguard against another hospital stay.

My mood had dipped into a severe depression. I knew that I had to try and pull myself out of this.

The benefit of my experience of lithium toxicity was that I managed to lose a lot of weight. I would not recommend duplicating that, I could have died after all! The by-product of this, was that my angina symptoms had disappeared altogether.

After speaking to my doctor, I was amazingly given the all clear to start running again, gradually. I began with the NHS couch to 5k program. I found the program a lot harder than I had expected, but I stuck with it and with fantastic support by Kathleen and Erin, I graduated the course with a 5k run at Watchtree nature reserve. It was harder work as it should have been and I was over twelve minutes slower than back when I was fitter, but it felt so good to have made what seemed like a massive step forward to a return to running.

Stilt Sandpiper in Northumberland

Juvenile Citrine Wagtail at Longtown

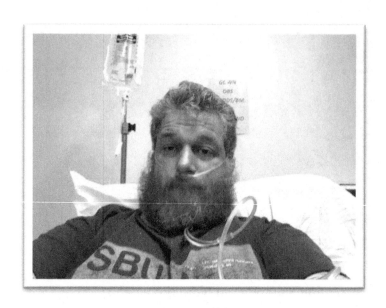

Me, looking unwell in hospital.

Happier times

Act Eight
Anxiety Tsunami

I was familiar with anxiety, mostly of the social flavour, and that was hard to cope with. What followed, not long after my lithium toxicity, was a level of fear, like I have never felt before! I don't know what specifically triggered this horrible period, but I would guess that the sudden reduction of lithium in my blood, probably added fuel to the situation. I am not a fearful or paranoid person, I can be a bit of an over thinker at times, but this was on another level all together.

There were a couple of events that happened which did cause a massive escalation of my already severe symptoms. These were a mass shooting in southern England and a murder in Carlisle. In reaction to the mass shooting, my mind constantly cycled a multitude of scenarios that all ended with the death of my family. Whenever I saw a person or car that I did not recognise or heard a strange noise, my panic levels would go through the metaphorical roof. The murder in Carlisle resorted in the prime suspects fleeing the scene and going on the run. This caused my fear levels to rise beyond any control. I was convinced my whole family were in imminent danger, sensible security measured went a bit crazy.

The doors and windows had to be always locked, I would check the garden for people hiding multiple times before I could do anything. I would look in the back garden through our kitchen window to make sure there was no one there. On several occasions I saw people hiding under a hedge. This was absolutely terrifying for me at the time. Although with hindsight I am certain that there were no people hiding under the hedge, it was very clear and very real to me at the time though. I do not know if these hallucinations were a direct result of my condition, but I have not experienced very many similar instances since. What I was experiencing was an irrational fear response to something happening in my brain. I was petrified that something so tragic was going to happen, that I could feel it in my body. It wasn't just a racing heartbeat; it was pain across my body and that was like that intense wired feeling that you can get from drinking too much coffee.

For some reason dreadful things often come in threes. The third prong to my suffering was paranoia. I tend to base what I believe or how I feel about things on what the evidence says. That seems the most logical and sensible approach to me! Of course, in my situation at the time, being logical or being sensible was an impossibility. A lot of my paranoia was focussed on my relationship with Kath. Admittedly, I am not the most self-assured person, but at this point, it seemed my self-esteem was most definitely missing in action. I was paranoid that Kath was having an affair. I was paranoid she would not care if I died. I was paranoid that she did not want to be with me anymore. None of this was true, but at the time that how I felt, and it was horrible. I tried to deal with this the best I could, but I became needy and requiring constant reassurance. It was hard going, because the force of the negative feeling I was immersed in was horribly strong. None of this was me. The strange, unexpected glimmer of positivity I can take from this very negative episode is that it caused Kath and I to talk more than we were, and that has strengthened our relationship. This problem went on for weeks and months and it was exhausting. I was struggling with sleep and during my plentiful waking hours my mind was cluttered with rapidly racing horrific intrusive thoughts. I started planning ways to end it permanently, mostly involving taking all my prescribed medication at once. It was one of the worse times of my life, but thankfully it did not come to that.

After an appointment with my psychiatrist, we discussed my symptoms and we decided to try an additional antidepressant that was also used to treat anxiety. Taking antidepressants when you have bipolar can be risky, so this was closely monitored. This additional medication really has worked and so far, I have had no similar anxiety episodes since. My anxiety symptoms are still present, like a whisper in the background rather than screaming in my ears like before. I also learned that I had to avoid watching the news, so I could sidestep any potential triggers.

Although I have already mentioned some of the problems I have encountered with my healthcare with the NHS, I do think that overall, I have been quite fortunate with the majority of the mental health professionals that have looked after me. For example, my psychiatrist has been exceptional, and this next account demonstrates this perfectly.

Alongside medicinal therapy, various applications of talking therapy were used to attempt to help to manage my bipolar symptoms. I had a lot of sessions with a psychotherapist where cognitive behavioural therapy modules were worked through, as well as Eye Movement Desensitisation and Reprocessing therapy (EDMR) and some trauma therapy. The latter therapy was abandoned as my psychotherapist felt that I was too unwell to cope with it. Overtime.

I built up a good rapport and a lot of trust with her. This is about to go dark very quickly. Living with bipolar seems to be a constant struggle, so in my personal experience, dark thoughts are always in reach. One morning I woke up and I felt energised and positive.

189

This was a sure sign of mania! Do you know when you have a fantastic plan, a fool proof plan and it will solve all your problems? Well, I had that very plan and it focused on my death. Living with bipolar is horrible at times, most of the time for me at least. The main things that stop me from taking that sharp exit is the impact it would likely have on my children. With my newfound logic, I came to the strong opinion that my kids would understand why I had to take my life if I explained my reasoning to them. They wouldn't want me to keep suffering unnecessarily, would they? I was feeling quite excited that I could finally be free.

As it happened, later that day I had an appointment with my psychotherapist. At my session I shared my very logical plan with her. I was expecting support and understanding, but that did not happen. I got reminded the impact my death from suicide would have on my kids, I was told that if I discussed my plans with my children, she would have to inform the child services and I would also probably have my kids taken from me. My GP was also alerted to my plans. This reaction sent me into the longest and worse period of depression I'd ever had. I felt so trapped, being stuck in my own brain with no escape.

Not long after this, my psychotherapist started the process of discharging me from the community mental health service. My mental health was the worst it had been, I wanted to die, yet she felt it was acceptable to discharge me. This made no sense to me then and it still doesn't now. Thankfully, my psychiatrist stepped in and stopped the process of me leaving the service. This quite possibly saved my life, though I'm not sure how grateful I am of that on my bad days!

Having a second chance at running was certainly helping me manage my mental and physical health a little better. As you would expect, it wasn't all plain sailing and there are always bumps in the road. I had spent a large part of late winter and spring training for the inaugural Grasmere Gallop marathon. I lined up on the start line, not feeling overconfident, but I was convinced that I would get myself around the course. I had no idea! I was moving around the very tough route far too slowly. By the time I hit the halfway point, I had missed the cut off time, so, sadly it was another DNF. I was disappointed with this result, but I knew that with my level of fitness, it was a case of too much too soon.

I continued training on the fells during the summer, I had another event on the horizon! Originally, I had signed up to the Brathay Ambleside 25k version of this event, then I got overconfident and 'upgraded' to the 50k. However, as I got closer to the race date, I realised I wasn't quite ready for that distance or elevation, so I sensibly (for once) returned to my original plan of running the 25k.

It was a beautiful route, but hugely challenging, I was pleased I had opted for the 25k eventually. Although it was a relatively short race, it felt like the hardest event I had ever participated in. This may have been more to do with my fitness level than anything else. The feeling of crossing the finish line of such a brutal race was phenomenal. The bonus was I was back in time to see Kath complete the 50k race.

A few weeks later and I was at a vastly different event! I had not specifically trained for any big mileage at this stage of the year, so what chance did I have of achieving anything significant? Thankfully, I did have some experience of the Watchtree NR 100mph 24hr, so I knew what the challenge entailed. My primary target was to go beyond 44 miles, though I did have a nice round figure of 100k (62 miles) niggling in the back of my mind, but I wasn't certain this was achievable for me. 11am came and a fair few of us set off in a clockwise direction. My pace was a little optimistic for the first loop, so I slowed it down on subsequent laps. This event was a positive experience, everyone encouraging each other as they passed on the course. The first few hours were enjoyable, it was nice seeing familiar faces and new ones. Kath and our older two girls were also on the reserve, giving me a boost early on. After a quick stop for some much needed food with Kath, I said my good-byes and continued plodding around the reserve. Morag and Dave were always awesome to see at the checkpoint, giving enthusiastic encouragement and checking we were all okay.

As I got deeper into the afternoon it was great to see Linda from Wigton Road Runners, who was not only contributing a few laps, but also helping with the event. Later, Linda was joined by Michelle (also from WRR) who both kindly accompanied me for a few laps. At this point I was 10 hours into the 24 and feeling surprisingly good. I did have some aches and pains as would be expected, but I was pleased that although I could feel it, my plantar fasciitis didn't seem to be getting any worse.

As the light faded, I was treated to a stunning sunset on the nature reserve. As darkness fell, I knew the game would change. I was pleased to have survived the first period of daylight, but now I had the dark hours to contend with. I was grateful to be joined by Kath, our three girls and Charlee (our springer spaniel) for three of the laps in the early darkness. This made an enormous difference mentally and set my routine for the rest of the night. I think, because I was only on the periphery of the nature reserve wildlife sightings were very rare. So, a couple of nocturnal newt sightings were a real bonus.

In the small hours of the night, I hit 46 miles, meaning I was now in unknown territory. I had a notion to continue until I'd covered 62 miles (100k). Dave quite rightly calmed me down and told me to take it a step at a time. Although few people stayed throughout the night it was great to see a few friendly faces. For most of the event I was running clockwise laps, while most people favoured the anticlockwise direction. This suited me fine as I could see who I was passing in the most part. There was a group of three that I got chatting to, they were pushing for 52 miles in the 24 hours, basically 2 marathons. It was great seeing them regularly and they were hugely encouraging and supportive of my effort.

192

They succeeded in their goal, I am pleased to say. Another person that stood out to me was Anna, she was covering laps at a phenomenal rate and every time she passed me, she always had something positive and encouraging to say. Anna finished her monster effort at around 6am and had covered a phenomenal 60 miles, to give some sort of context, I had 'only' covered 52 miles at that point.

I was surprised that my imagination did not go too wild during the hours of darkness. That said, when Morag ran past me in the dark my head torch picked up the reflective strips on her running tights and I was convinced that she was riding a tiny unicycle! Sam had sent me messages of support the previous evening and it was fantastic to get a call from him as the light crept in. This certainly spurred me on to continue the plod.

So how hard was it physically to keep going? Well to be honest, not terrible. My plantar fasciitis discomfort appeared to have disappeared but was replaced by quite bad leg pain. Once I had convinced myself that the pain wasn't going to kill me, I was able to keep going. I have to say that it was more comfortable to run than it was to walk, so I did far more running than I expected to be able to do.

When the daylight came in so did more participants, this gave me a boost as it was great seeing some familiar faces from the previous day (like Vicky from WRR) and some new ones (like Kath's twin). So much encouragement from people. It was so nice that Linda, Michelle, and Sharon joined me for my last few laps, I really appreciated the enthusiastic support. As I finished what I decided was my final lap I was absolutely elated to be greeted by fantastic applause and congratulations. At 22hrs 40mins I had somehow hit my dream target of 62 miles.

Now I've had time to process what I achieved; I am quite pleased. That said I have learned a lot of lessons and I know there is huge room for improvement, but considering I didn't specifically train for the distance and I'm a fat lad in his late 40's that has no business trying to run an ultra-distance, 62 miles isn't too shabby!

In early January, I started being coached by Paul Wilson of Summit Ultra Coaching courtesy of a Christmas gift from Kath. I have known Paul for a good number of years, so I was already aware of his incredible credentials and personality. I was super stoked to have the opportunity to be guided by him with my training and race strategy. I accepted that I was not his usual type of client, I am slow, fat and have serious mental health issues, but I knew Paul liked a challenge! So, my aim for all the events I had entered was not to be super-fast or competitive but to beat the cut-offs and finish in reasonable condition physically.

I must admit that running to a carefully curated plan took a bit of getting used to, but I quickly became committed to the process. Knowing that each training session is for a specific reason helps for sure, I began enjoying my running a lot more. Not long after starting my coaching with Paul, I had signed up for a race with Fellside Events. The event was a short 4.4-mile trail race starting in Brampton. I knew that I wouldn't be benefiting much from my training by that point, so my main aim was to get around, enjoy it and give a good account of myself. It was more of a benchmark than anything else.

It was great to be back in a trail race environment again and nice to catch up with a few folks I hadn't seen for a while. This was also my middle-daughter Erin's first race, so quite exciting! The plan was to start at an easy pace with Erin and see how it went. After the race briefing, we lined up at the start and the race began. Rightly or wrongly, we started at the back and after running through the starting field we began the first little (but relatively steep) climb up to the monument. We took it easy until reaching a bit of a bottleneck near the top where we were forced to slow to a walk. As we continued, we re-joined the main track and then onto some fields before entering the woodland.

We did manage to pass a few runners in this section which was good. I sensed that Erin could move faster and as I didn't want to hold her back, I suggested she could run on without me, so she did exactly that. It was fantastic running on the muddy trails, through the woodlands and fields. The marshals were all fantastic and encouraging. By the time I arrived at the road at the halfway point I was feeling good. I didn't feel the need to stop at the water station, so I continued running up the hill before re-joining the trails back up to the woodland. Then it was a short run along the fields before a nice downhill finish. It was great to see Kath, Erin, and Sam as I crossed the finish line, all three had a great race. I was pleased with my race, I knew I was slow compared to most of the field, but I felt like I was consistent. I was pleased to have enough in the tank for an old school sprint finish!

For the next few weeks, I continued with my running schedule with an eye on my next race, which was the Greener Miles Whinlatter Moonrunner 10k. This race was postponed from the previous December due to dangerous weather conditions. As the name suggests this was a night/head-torch event along the trails at Whinlatter Forest Park. I had not trained specifically for this race as my main focus was my first 'A' race of the year, the Grasmere Gallop Marathon. That said, I was very much looking forward to the race, I just was not expecting an amazing performance.

The day or should I say night had come and I found myself lining up at the start. After the race briefing, I said good luck to Kath and positioned myself near the back of the runners. The race started and I began the first long climb up along the forest trails. That first climb was just shy of a mile long and although not horrendously steep, it was still a challenge. I knew there was a far harder climb to come, so took this first mile easy. Night running on trails is relatively new to me, but I have been doing it a fair bit throughout the dark winter months. I really enjoy the experience; it certainly adds another dimension to my running.

The first mile was a bit harder than I expected, but I stuck to my plan and was surprisingly able to pass a few participants. Once I got to the top of the climb, I knew it was around two miles of downhill. So, I was able to pick up the pace, knowing the toughest section was ahead, I knew I couldn't go flat out. I settled into a reasonable pace and really enjoyed the downhill. I even managed to gain a few more places. Once I hit a more technical section, I got caught behind a couple who were not as confident on the dark trails as I seemed to be, so I was forced to slow down. This was okay by me as I needed to save something for the immanent climb.

Once I reached the lowest elevation of the route it was time to begin the pretty brutal and technical two mile climb up to Seat How. I struggle with climbs, I tend to move very slowly, so this is where I expected to be passed by those runners I had overtaken on the downhill. I was totally amazed that this did not happen, I was still in the same position as I made it to the top.

Perhaps I was getting a little stronger with all this training. I was running behind a couple in the last of the proper technical terrain, but I was able to pass them once we reached the main track again. I was into the last mile of the race, and it was all downhill, I just hoped I had left enough in my legs to make the most of it. As I pushed on, I realised I could finish strong. I saw a group of three runners ahead of me and I was beginning to gain on them. Conscious that there was a narrower slightly technical section coming up, I was quite keen to pass the runners sooner rather than later. So, I put my foot down and cruised past them. One runner in that group seemingly wasn't keen on my fat unit passing him and he also put the pedal to the metal. It felt like he was close behind me as I ran down through the trees, but as determined as he was to pass me, I think I must have been more determined that he didn't.

After increasing my pace, I managed to drop him and ran into the finish unchallenged!

I enjoyed the race and felt I executed it well. There is huge room for improvement, but isn't there always? I can certainly claim improvement compared to the Fellside Events Brampton Trail Race in January; a better grade adjusted pace seems a good indication at least. My unrealistic target was sub-80 minutes, which I did not achieve, however I did manage to hit my more realistic secondary target of sub-90 minutes. So happy days!

Not long after the Whinlatter race I had sunk into one of the worse depressive episodes I'd had in the previous few years, and I was struggling to cope, I definitely needed help. I was also continuing to have problems sleeping, which was exacerbating my symptoms. My CPN quickly organised an appointment with my psychiatrist which was the intervention I needed. The psychiatrist gave me a few options that he believed would help me. After a bit of discussion, we agreed on adding in the Phenylpiperazine antidepressant, Trazodone. Given that I already take Sertraline (a serotonin reuptake inhibitor antidepressant) along with Lithium, my psychiatrist believed that Trazodone would not only help me sleep and ease the depression, but also it was not likely to trigger a manic (or hypomanic) episode.

Whilst all this nasty stuff was happening everything in my life stopped functioning, everything except running, which was amazing. In fact, since I had started running with a coach, I had not missed a training session. Considering what I was dealing with and how I was feeling, I am proud of that fact. When you deal with this horrible psychiatric disorder, you have got to accept the wins, however insignificant they may seem.

Here's where events get a little grey. I started taking the Trazodone and titrating up to a therapeutic dose. The medication was beginning to have a positive affect as although I was still depressed, I was feeling a significant amount better.

The best way I can explain this, was I had a low mood, but I no longer had my head full of darkly dark thoughts. I was starting to find enjoyment in things again, and I was looking forward to and enjoying my training a lot more. So, things were going well. Then one morning I woke up feeling a little different. I had felt like this before, but not for a couple of years. It was a nice feeling, the depression seemed to have had been replaced with a super-hyped and energised mood. You would have thought I would have recognised what was happening, having been in this situation countless times before, but I rarely recognise it when I'm in amongst it! I went about my day, and I felt great. I tend to get very spendy when my mind is like this.

However, as a family we have learnt by my previous mistakes, and I no longer have access to our main finances. It makes me feel like a child at times, but I know it is necessary. I did have some of my own money of course, though it was just a small amount. As you will know by now, I tend to get obsessed with some things when I'm like this. This time for some unknown reason I got obsessed with nutrition. I ended purchasing a three-month supply of Huel meal replacement powders, this is a product that I've never had any interest in before. I also bought a box of Mountain Fuel energy gels; despite the fact I have not used gels to fuel my running for about eight years. It seems stupid now, but at the time it was part of a bigger plan. So, my day progressed, and I was still oblivious to what state I was in. I did not sleep well that night, but I really did not feel like I needed to. I got up the next morning feeling great, in fact I was well and truly wired. The day's obsession was creating running routes on the fantastic running and hiking route making app, Kamoot.

The first route I created, was the 'Ambleside T-Round.' As the name suggests it starts in Ambleside in the Lake District and connects the summits of all the Wainwright's that start with letter T. With 115 miles (185 km) and over 22,000 feet (6,706 meters) of ascent this challenging route was the tamest of adventures I would plan over the next day or so.

Do you see where we are going here? I was super excited about this adventure, but soon became focused on another running round. This one I named 'the Pikes Round.' Yes, you have guessed it, this one starts in Hesket Newmarket and connects all the Wainwright's with the word pike in their name. At 141 miles (227 km) and over 42,000 feet (13,411 meters) of ascent this was a true monster of a challenge. Amongst many other incredible things, Kath is my voice of reason and stability. Once I had chatted to her for some time, she stopped me and asked me if I was sure I wasn't manic because grandiose plans were a big red flag for this. I said no, but I knew she was right. This caused my mood to drop like a stone, back into a state of depression. This was an unusual situation for me, manic or hypomanic episodes have always lasted for weeks or months previous, not just a few days. All very strange.

The following few days were back to normal, not great but more what I was used too. Then Thursday arrived and I woke up feeling fantastic, this was not a good sign. I got myself immersed in Kamoot again, creating multiple versions of the same general route. This one was a serious one though, making my previous routes look very tame. Rationality had gone on a vacation, and I had planned two routes from Lands' End to John O' Groats following predominantly trails rather than the usual roads. I was super hyped about this and was fairly convinced this project was achievable for me, very soon. Who needs sleep! Later in the day I had my usual five to six mile fell or trail run planned. Given the wintry conditions we decided to go to Binsey, one of the smaller wainrights. I had become obsessed with running up and down the fell four times at least via various route choices.

I was really excited about doing this, despite the weather and despite none of our group sharing my enthusiasm. It was supposed to be an easy effort run! On arrival it was snowing lightly, but there was a fair bit under foot too. It was also quite windy, which added to the experience. Kath insisted that we only did one ascent, I begrudgingly compromised to two ascents. The conditions were challenging, but it felt incredibly epic to be there. Once we got to the summit Kath insisted, we ran back down to the car, I was uncharacteristically oblivious to the welfare and safety of anyone else (including myself) and after a tense exchange I started running off the back of the fell to enable our second climb. At the halfway mark, Kath sternly insisted that we went back up the fell and back down to the car. I felt very agitated, but I really had no choice. In hindsight and with my rational brain engaged, I know Kath was making sure everyone was safe, and I am grateful for that.

It is quite painful looking back on my behaviour even though I had no control over it at the time. Bipolar Disorder is recognised as a progressive illness, so perhaps these short cycles of hypomania could be attributed to deterioration of the disorder. I hoped not, but I guess time will tell. Another contributing factor could be the change in the season, this can trigger the manic side of the illness and has done in the past, though this is usually in early spring.

The obvious elephant in the room was the introduction of the new medication, trazodone. I really hoped this was not the causal factor. Thankfully, any reactions caused by the medication were short lived, and I am still able to take it now, with no ill effects.

I was continuing to get a lot of enjoyment out of my training which has been helpful for me mentally. It gave me motivation to get out the door when I was not feeling too energised. Also, improvement, really made putting on my running shoes a lot more worthwhile. I had been specifically training for a familiar event, the Grasmere Gallop Marathon. The main purpose of the training block was to get me to the start line of my second attempt at the very tough marathon in better physical condition than the previous year.

I felt more prepared for this marathon than I had been for any of my previous ones. Unfortunately, due to the very hot conditions I was losing more fluids than I could take onboard. Some of the medications I have to take affect my body's ability to thermoregulate efficiently, so this coupled with the dehydration potentially causing the lithium levels in my blood to reach toxic levels, added some additional concerns and complexity. To cut a long story short, I failed to finish this trail marathon for the second year running. Frustrating, but you can only ever do your best on the day. At least I got to join Erin to cheer in Kath and her cousin Alison who had both ran a fantastic race.

After a bit of self-pity, followed by discussions with Paul and Kath I came to the realisation that I was doing things wrong! I really enjoyed the training blocks up to an event, but I didn't enjoy the pressure of the race. Due to having to take medications that restrict the upper end of my heart rate, pace is something with which I would always struggle. My weight was a factor in this too, but that was heading in the right direction at the time. The conclusion I came to after considering all of that, was to stop doing races and organised events, at least for now, and focus on giving the multitude of rounds and point to points available in the Lake District and beyond a go. This would mean that I could train for an adventure knowing that there are no time constraints, so not only would I be able have a better chance of successfully completing a challenge, but the lack of pressure would make it a lot more enjoyable. I just want to run in beautiful places, after all!

After discussing things in a bit more depth with Paul, we agreed that we should do one of the smaller rounds to make the most of the recent training block. We decided on the Fishers Espresso Round, a twelve-mile route that starts and finishes in Keswick and takes in four peaks between Derwentwater and Braithwaite village. That sounded like fun!

The day arrived and Paul picked me up from my home and we made the short trip into Keswick. Once we arrived at George Fishers, the start point, we activated our watches and began the adventure. As we ran through the town and along the footpath towards Portinscale, I was feeling a little nervous.

There were absolutely no time pressures here, but I still wanted to give a reasonable account of myself. For some reason or other, in recent runs, my legs did not seem to have much to give, this was possibly a hangover from my recent Grasmere Gallop Marathon DNF.

Whatever the reason, I took the flat run along Derwentwater at a steadier pace than usual, particularly as there were some big climbs to come. Before long we were climbing the rocky path towards Catbells. This fell is probably the most popular mountain in the Lake District, the well-worn path seems to be testament to that. As we had set off early, the route up was not too busy. I hadn't been up this fell for over nine years, and I had forgotten how rocky and rugged the long climb up was. After the scramble up to the lower peak of Skelgill Bank, it was a continued, but reasonable climb before the rocky scramble onto the Catbells summit.

The views from this iconic mountain were breathtaking, making the challenging work to get there very worthwhile. Interestingly the name 'Catbells' is thought to be a distortion of 'Cat Bields' that means 'Shelter of the wildcat.' At 1,480 ft (451m) elevation, this fell was not the highest peak we would climb up to on the route, but it gave us a commanding view of our target fells for the morning. With summit trig tagged, we descended the rocky outcrop to pick up a path that took us into the valley to Stair. It was a lovely day for it, still quite warm, but a scattering of short light showers cooled things down from time to time. The steep and quite technical climb up to Rowling End, was hard graft and I was feeling like I was experiencing type two, or maybe type three fun! I found the climb a lot tougher than I should have, so I was moving very slowly.

My mind was in a pretty negative place at this point, but Paul reassured me by reminding me that time was irrelevant and to remember to enjoy where we were. This helped me plod on! It was great to touch the summit of Rowling End and soak up the views back towards Catbells and across the ridge to the next fell top on our route, the very distinctive Causey Pike. It was manageable terrain underfoot from Rowling End towards Causey Pike, until an intense steep rocky climb up to the buttress below the summit, after another minor rock scramble we were on top of Causey Pike, at 2,090 ft (637m) it was the highest point on the round. It felt great to know we had completed the toughest section of the route. The views were unreal too!

Next, we took a steep challenging line off the mountain towards Stonycroft Gill, before the last and gentlest climb of the adventure up to summit four of the adventure, Barrow. It was a great feeling standing on the final mountain of the route, knowing it was downhill or flat running to the finish. After the descent to the lodge, I realised just how destroyed my legs were! It was a slow slog back to Portinscale and into a busy Keswick to George Fishers and the finish of the Espresso Round. Considering how bad I was feeling going up Rowling End, I was ecstatic that I had completed this challenge. It would not have been achievable without Paul, for which I will always be grateful.

I know for most seasoned fell and ultra runners, this route would be no big deal, but for me personally, given my health and mental baggage, this was a huge personal achievement. It felt good to have completed such a big challenge, my first since I was able to return to running. Paul had really got me through this one! This new approach to running was certainly making my training far more enjoyable, although it did still come with some frustrations.

I had used a social media platform called Strava for many years to log my runs. This was a fantastic way to share adventures and interact with other athletes. The app and website give users a breakdown of their run data, showing metrics like mile (or kilometre) pace, fitness score, heart rate and average pace. The adage 'comparison is the thief of joy' has become very relevant to me here. I have never compared my performance to other athletes, I've never been that competitive, or quick enough to warrant it! The problem I had since my return to running has been comparing my old performances to my new ones. This left me so frustrated with my current performance that I failed to see the small yet significant improvements I was making. That average pace metric can be a double-edged sword! Any sensible person would identify the problem and remove it, but for me, this really was not an option. I was too invested into Strava to let it disappear. The application had a record of almost every run I had ever done, along with all my mileage stats, personal bests and a lot more besides. So, my only option was just to not care about how my runs looked to other people. So far, this is working quite well.

Thea always had a fearless interest in insects!

Thea and Erin keeping warm on a stormy evening on Brae Fell whilst helping to marshal the Fellside Fell Race.

The trio on the top of Dodd, with Charlee.

The five of us, all looking a lot younger!

A happy Tristan, having completed the Ambleside 25k trail race.

Views from Catbells

Me and Paul on Barrow, the final summit on the Espresso Round

Act Nine
Music Therapy

Mary Gore has a lot to be thanked for, since she pushed to have 'Parental Advisory' stickers placed onto any music that was deemed to contain 'unsuitable content.' In my younger years I used this as a guide of what I should listen to. If it has that 'Parental Advisory' emblazoned on the front cover, then I was going to give it a listen! I never admit to continuing to pick my music based on that rule now though...

Whilst trying to find my way through secondary school I started to explore heavy metal, from the glam-rock and subsequent blues-rock of Cinderella to the unapologetic thrash metal of Slayer. I liked the energy and storytelling, it was loud and angry, something that I needed then and even now, sometimes. Not only did I enjoy the escapism of the music, but it gave me a little connection so some of my colleagues at school.

During my latter years I at school, I introduced myself to the culture of hip-hop. This was a whole new world of amazing graffiti artwork, breakdancing, popping and of course rap music. The first rap music I listened to was NWA's seminal gangsta' rap album 'Straight Outta Compton.' This music was a huge education for me, as a white boy living in Cornwall, this music was my introduction to white versus black prejudice and racism. People would focus on the graphic lyrics and get offended, but they were missing the point. What Ice Cube, Eazy-E, Dr Dre, Arabian Prince, and the rest were actually doing was holding up a giant megaphone to make sure we knew what real life was like living in the neighbourhoods of Compton. This was powerful storytelling, and it would have a very big impact on my life.

My musical preference, I never seemed to tie myself rigidly to one genre in particular. would be best described as eclectic As with many aspects of my life, I was always attracted to the unusual when it came to music, and I wasn't averse to taking a risk. I would often by EP's and LP's from imports or artists I'd never heard of. This practice introduced me to bands like Dogs D'Amour and Molly half-head.

Perhaps some early evidence of my obsessive symptoms was fuelled by my passion for music. I started buying pre-owned 'entertainment centres' from charity shops. These had a turntable and a tape deck; these were the ones that were popular in the seventies. Not content with two speakers, I would often wire in two or four extra. It was not unusual for me to cause the odd explosion due to my amateur electrical work.

Once I had my rig safely set up, I needed music to play on it. I would return to the charity shops to sift through the vinyl on sale in the hope of finding some gems. I found great music by some varied artists like Carter USM, Bob Marley and Misty in Roots! Once I started college, I had become obsessed with the music of Bob Dylan! Admittedly not to everyone's taste and even I used to hate when my father used to play it in my younger years. For some reason, I started choosing to listen to Bob Dylan when I was around fifteen years old. I really liked his uniqueness, humour and amazing story telling. This new interest triggered a single-minded obsession to purchase as many Bob Dylan albums as I could find. I ended up with his entire back catalogue, including those dodgy ones from his religious phase! This was all I would listen to for months on end.

The group that shocked me back to a more open-minded taste in music was the politically charged American rock band, Rage Against the Machine. The frustrated voice of Zack de la Rocha and the guitar brilliance of Tom Morello made for a breathtaking combination. This mixture of metal and hip-hop was exactly what I never knew I was searching for! I soon learned that this new genre of music was referred to as nü-metal. I would soon be introduced to the purposefully vacuous music of Limp Bizkit, the angry angst of Papa Roach and the hugely atmospheric sound of Linkin Park. This was certainly a varied genre, and one I still dive into today.

It wasn't all about vinyl and compact disks, live music would feature prominent during this period of my life. I should tell you that I had experienced live music back when I was working at Paradise Park. We had a Christmas outing to see Status Quo, not really my sort of music, but it was a really good night.

When I was living in Perthshire, I spent many a night at a pub and music venue called the Twa Tams. This pub would often host 'up and coming' bands as well as new talent and older 'used to be popular' bands! I cannot remember every band I did see, but I certainly enjoyed seeing Long Fin Killie, The Sensational Alex Harvey Band (minus Alex Harvey, sadly), The Fall and if I'm remembering correctly, The Bluestone. They were good times!

Whichever music genre I was focussing on, hip-hop was never very far away. Having started listening to NWA, I began listening to other lyrical rappers such as Lauryn Hill, LL Cool J, Rakim, Big Daddy Kane, Q-tip and the group, Public Enemy. Nothing prepared me for the lyrical juggernaut of Eminem! This rapper had writing and rapping skills like I'd never heard before, not since Rakim at least. No-one could compare in my opinion.

Eminem's lyrics were not for the feint hearted; he was rapping about his tough start to life living on a trailer park in Detroit with abusive parents. His lyrics could be very amusing and entertaining, equally they could be visceral and graphic. The more I listened to his music, the more I saw double, and frequently triple meanings. The broadness of his vocabulary and his ability to bend words in his rhymes took his ability to tell a story to a level above most other rappers at the time. I spent a long time disappearing into the warped world of Slim Shady, and I still do.

I found out from quite a young age that music allowed me to disappear into another world, giving me some escape from the difficulties of my personal life. However, there was a contrary side to this. Having stopped listening to music for many years after my bipolar symptoms became very difficult to manage. During therapy, it was suggested that I should maybe listen to music again to help me relax a bit better. Perhaps Eminem wasn't my best choice for this! After a look on my music streaming services, I was excited to see that Eminem was still making music, and quite prolifically. I got quite obsessed with this and decided I couldn't listen to the new work until I had listened to everything Marshal Mathers had made, and in chronological order. A few days later and some twenty-odd albums consumed, and I'd done it! I have done similar with the Ukrainian metalcore band, Jinjer and the Swedish rock band, The Hives.

These obsessive behaviours can almost certainly be attributed to my bipolar symptoms, I think that they can be considered benign, as they are of no harm to myself or anyone else.

Music is still a very important part of my life, and on the whole, I can keep things fairly balanced. I use music predominantly as a form of mindfulness, if I'm struggling with depression, I will sometimes put on some Eminem, Rage Against the Machine, Lincoln Park or something completely different. It definitely helps, even if only for a short while.

Act Ten
Challenge

Having successfully completed the short, yet, challenging, George Fisher's Espresso Round, a new challenge was needed to focus my training towards. After chatting through some ideas and options with my coach, we decided I would take on the George Fisher's Tea Round! This round was formally known as the Abraham's Tea Round, because the route was based on all the peaks visible from Abraham's Café that was situated in the floor above the outdoor supplies shop, George Fisher. However, the Keswick based cafe has since closed down and been replaced, which is why the rounds name has been changed to the George Fisher's Tea Round.

The rules of the challenge are quite straightforward, prospective runners will start and finish at the doors of the George Fisher shop and ensure they take in the peaks of the ten fells. This can be ran or walked in any order or direction, though there is a suggested route that is recommended to try and reduce erosion on the trails and trods. The challenge is currently supported by the outdoor clothing brand, Montane, so runners or walkers who successfully complete the round are offered a commemorative t-shirt.

At the time of considering the challenge, I was quite familiar with seven of the ten required peaks. Thankfully, the route was relatively close to home, so I knew I would have the opportunity to recce all of the route during the imminent training block! The mountain summits that need to be tagged in this round were Catbells, Robinson, High Stile, Whiteless Pike, Hobcarton Crag, Grisedale Pike, Crag Hill, Sail Fell, Scar Crags, Causey Pike, Rowling End and Barrow. The length of the route is estimated to be 31 miles (50 km), with over 10,000 feet (3,058 meters) of elevation gain. This challenge was going to be a big ask of my barely cooperative body!

Here is an interesting snippet, one of those fells mentioned is home to a very rare wildflower. The species is Alpine Catchfly, and it is only found at one other location in the UK. Unfortunately, due to the general stupidity and greed of some humans, at the Cumbrian location the plants are quite difficult to see, as they only grow high up on the mountains steep side. The one time I have seen the Alpine Catchfly there, I had to use a telescope to get worthwhile views! Unfortunately, I cannot give any details on the location of this botanical gem, as I would be hunted down by hordes of angry botanists!

I knew the George Fisher's Tea Round was way too big for me, but with no time limit and some solid training, I thought that it might just be possible. The training block was full on, as you would expect, given the goal. With a good mix of structured running sessions, strength, and conditioning workouts, and plenty of time on the trails and fells, it was certainly never boring. During my long run on the weekend, I would plan routes either on the route or on closer fells, either way, there would be plenty of long climbs guaranteed! I loved having the ability to get out in the fells, but I was finding the climbs exceedingly difficult. This would constantly chip away at my confidence and have me questioning whether I could get around the Tea Round or even question why I was even trying. I was following the training plan that Paul had devised for me and putting as much effort as I could into it. However, I didn't seem to notice any significant improvements in my climbing. There were measurable improvements in other areas of my running, just not where any elevation was concerned. This was frustrating, and I knew I had to work out what the root cause was.

The obvious elephant in the room was the fact that I was overweight, resolving this was always a complex work in progress and the progress was always slow. Basic physics tells us that the more you weigh the slower you will be able to run, so this was obviously a significant factor. I knew I had run quicker on hills when I was a lot heavier, this suggested to me that there was more to consider.

I looked at how I felt physically when attempting to move efficiently up hills and what I identified was that on any incline at all, my legs felt awful. They felt like they had no fuel in them, they felt sore and useless. I did consider that it might have been a progression of the neurological condition that had been diagnosed when I was a child. However, I became convinced that the most likely cause was related to the medication that restricts the upper end of my heart rate that I had to take. This made a lot of sense, if my heart rate cannot go high enough to get oxygen to me legs, I would not have the climbing engine I needed! This was very frustrating, but it was very much, a reality. Sometimes you must accept the tools you have got. For someone who has had to fight against a lot of things in their life, this was a tough ask. After some thought and internal discussion, I did what I knew I had to do and accept my situation. Although I did not know it at the time, this new approach to problems would be a game changer when it came to how I saw and learned to manage my bipolar symptoms.

During this training block I had logged over 470 miles (756 km) with at least 83,400 feet (25,420 meters) of climbing. This included reaching ninety fell summits (including repeat visits). This was the hardest I had ever trained for an event or challenge, but I had enjoyed every moment of it (almost)! I loved the fact that I was able to test myself in the mountains again.

As the day of my Tea Round attempt approached, I felt more prepared than I had ever felt. I was under no illusion though; it was going to be a massive challenge and a long day out. To say I was super hyped after finalising the date and logistics with Paul, was quite the understatement. The day arrived and Paul picked me up at around 5.15am, the weather conditions were far from ideal, but I was determined to get the job done. I had trained in extremely poor wet and windy conditions, so I felt like I was prepared for anything.

With that said I did question why I wanted to attempt this challenge in the first place. I knew it was not just so I could say that I'd done it, because that would be pointless. I wanted to do it to see what I was capable of, but most of all, I wanted to enjoy the adventure. Something I had noticed was that I put a lot of my energy into the build up to a challenge. Although there was nothing unusual about that, for me it was quite challenging. When you are already in energy deficit from navigating through a normal day, this added strain on your resources can only go one way. For these reasons, I had decided that if my attempt to run the Tea Round did not go as planned, I would postpone giving it another go until the summer months. This would mean there would be more of a chance of sunny weather, beautiful views, and longer hours of daylight. This all made perfect sense, for once! I chatted to Paul about this as we made our way to Keswick in the persistent rain, and he agreed with my recent epiphany! I suggested that if I didn't succeed with that day's challenge, I could make some use of the training block my running the Espresso Round again. He thought that would be a clever idea and proposed that maybe I should consider taking that on this time, instead of the Tea Round, given the nasty weather. Paul was not keen for me to be out of the fells for eighteen or so hours in rapidly deteriorating conditions. I could see that the risks could be potentially dangerous and the last thing I would want to do was put anyone else at risk if I needed to be rescued. You must respect the conditions particularly when you are in the mountains.

215

I agreed with Paul's suggestion and planned to run the Espresso Round.

Watch started and head torch on I set off through Keswick and onto Portinscale to run along the wooded trails that skirted Derwentwater. The shelter of the trees gave me a false perspective of the weather conditions, once I got out onto the slopes of Catbells the reality of the poor weather was inescapable. The light arrived when I was around halfway up the mountain, which made things a little easier. The persistent rain and increasing wind certainly sucked any enjoyment out of the adventure. The rocky scrambles were made even more challenging due to the slippery wet rocks. I was incredibly pleased to reach the summit as I knew I had a good chunk of downhill to look forward to. After the long descent to Scales, Paul met me again. We mutually agreed that the conditions were far too grim to make continuing a sensible option, so I gladly called my adventure off for the day!

Paul was super keen that I got something positive out of all my hard training and made the particularly good suggestion that I should consider running the thirty or so miles of the Cumbria Way path from Keswick to Carlisle sometime in the following few weeks. Given that I had running the full route of the Cumbria Way on my radar for some time soon, this seemed like the ideal solution to the situation. I was super excited about this and swiftly began planning this new adventure. This point-to-point route is more of a trail running adventure than a fell running one, although it would take me over High Pike just before the halfway point. This route wouldn't have the continuous climbing challenge that the Tea Round has, but the fact that it is more runnable would come with its own potential difficulty.

It was not long before Kath was dropping me off in Keswick just after 7.30am on a Saturday morning. The day had arrived, and I was about to see if my recent training block had given me the tools to complete the big challenge ahead. After getting my kit sorted and saying my good-byes to Kath, it was a short walk to the Moot Hall.

The Moot Hall is situated in the centre of Keswick. It was originally built to be used as a medieval courthouse, it has since gained iconic status in the fell running community because it marks the start and finish of legendary endurance rounds like the Bob Graham Round and the Steve Parr Round. I could have started my challenge at the bottom of Spoonygreen Lane, but it seemed fitting for me to pay homage to those incredible fell running achievements and start my big effort from the Moot Hall, particularly as realistically I was unlikely to have the physical ability to run any of those big rounds.

As it was market day in the town, getting to the hall was more challenging than I anticipated! I set off feeling positive about the adventure that was ahead of me. It was going to be a tough day on the trails, but I was uncharacteristically confident. It was a gentle run through the town and Fitz Park before the familiar climb up Spoonygreen Lane to the Gayle Road Carpark. It was a cold but beautiful morning with amazing views over the fells. I knew the first half of the route very well, so I was able to loosely gauge how I would need manage my pace and energy levels for the first ten miles or so. Whilst chatting with Kath before I set off, she gave some great advice, when she told me to remember you can only control the controllables.

This became my mantra whilst I was running on the Cumbria Way. My controllables during the run were nutrition, hydration and simply keeping moving forward, if I was consistent with all three of these, I knew I would have a good chance of success. After crossing Whit Beck in the shadow of Skiddaw, I followed the wide track as it gently climbed along the side of Lonscale to the gate. From there it was a nice undulating path with some varied terrain up to the Skiddaw House Hostel.

I was around six miles into my run at that point and I was still feeling incredibly good. I was aware what was going on with me here, but this was not a controllable, and besides, it was making the experience feel amazing, so it was really helping me! From Skiddaw House it was around four miles of quite rocky and boggy single-track path which was almost certainly the most scenic section of the route. Nearby Stonechats and Red Grouse along the way were a definite bonus.

At around ten miles in and I was beginning to steepest climb of the day following the Grainsgill Beck up to Lingy Hut. I must admit that when I first glanced the hut on the fell ahead of me, it seemed a lot further away than I had remembered! The climb was quite challenging, not just because I already had ten miles of trails in my legs, but because it was steep and both boggy and rocky, which certainly added to my experience. Perhaps, because I knew it was part of the biggest climb on the route, I was remaining positive and confident as I ascended towards Lingy Hut. It didn't seem long before I was running towards the hut. Lingy Hut is a remote bothy that is maintained by the Mountain Bothy Association (MBA) as well as local volunteers (including some from Northern Fells Running Club, of which I am a current member of). The hut is frequently used by hikers attempting to walk the Cumbria Way.

After passing Lingy Hut and joining the wider track it was another short climb onto the summit of High Pike. This was a mountain I was very familiar with having ran various routes to its summit for many years, both before and since my physical health meltdown!

On this day, High Pike was quite significant as it was not only the highest point of the route, but it also marked the end of the big climbs for the day. When I planned my route, I calculated that the full distance would be short of the 50k mark, so I knew I would need to make up the additional miles somewhere along the way. Originally, I thought I would add this onto the end of my run once I had reached Carlisle. However, I concluded that this plan would probably be quite soul destroying! What I opted to do was take a less direct route to Nether Row off High Pike. Having those extra miles on a downhill section seemed like a nice bonus.

After tagging the trig on High Pike I settled in to enjoy the descent to Nether Row at a purposefully slightly measured pace. From Nether Row it was a run down a road hill before crossing a couple of fields into Caldbeck. Sixteen miles in and I was feeling amazing! I visited the public toilets, to do my business (the only time I sat down during the whole run!) and grabbed a quick takeaway coffee (and a hot choc for Kath) before meeting up with my amazing crew in the village carpark. It was great to see Kath and our girls. Whilst Erin and Thea replenished my water bottles and disposed of my used gel packets, I was able to give Kath an update on how things had gone so far. She could not quite believe how fresh faced and positive I was, to be honest neither could I. I'd had a fairly efficient pit stop, so we made plans to meet at a point on the route between Dalston and Cummersdale and I was back out on the trail again. I was still on familiar ground as I ran through Caldbeck campsite and through the gate to Parsons Park. The trail follows the Cald Beck for a brief time before climbing up a little on muddy paths through a pleasant bit of broadleaf woodland. After a gentle descent I was on a flatter track that took me towards the river Caldew again and onto the small village of Sebergham. The next part of the route I was a little nervous about as I did not know it at all. However, I needn't have been worried at all, as the route was very obvious on the ground. After crossing the bridge in Sebergham I took the footpath left past the first house. After a little steep climb, the path took me past some properties before I joined the bridleway to Bell Bridge. This was a nice section underfoot and despite being twenty miles into my run, my legs allowed me to move quite efficiently still.

The miles were continuing to tick by without my notice and I was feeling exceptionally good both physically and mentally. The following section took me through farmland and parkland that followed the meandering River Caldew quite closely. There were quite a lot of livestock in many of the fields I traversed, so some care was required. This slowed me up a little, but this wasn't a massive concern as I was not chasing a time! The path took me to Rose Bridge and then past Limehouse School and into the town of Dalston. I picked up a drink here to top up my hydration. I had been using Mountain Fuel Sports Jelly+ (natural flavour) every thirty minutes consistently during my run, and they had been working very well for me. However, I think after six or seven hours, my stomach was beginning to protest! I decided to switch my nutrition to my tried and tested Voom bars for the remaining miles. I was now 27 miles in and quite remarkably feeling strong.

I called Kath and told her she did not need to catch me near Cummersdale as planned and I would see her at the Castle.

The rest of the route was on flat tarmacked paths. Now my legs were understandably feeling a bit sore by then, but nowhere near as bad as I had experienced on all my previous long-distance runs. I certainly hadn't entered the all too familiar pain cave, I was close, but I definitely did not check in! The final miles into Carlisle went well, I was surprisingly moving well. I was incredibly happy to see the mighty Carlisle Castle. I ran under the underpass before running up the steps to the castle entrance whilst getting amazing encouragement from Kath and our girls. I had only done it, the Moot Hall in Keswick to Carlisle Castle along the Cumbria Way, 32 amazing miles, what an incredible experience.

As I stood at the castle entrance soaking in what I had achieved, I was amazed with how good I felt. Could I have ran further, it certainly felt possible! I sent a message to my coach, saying I had finished, or words to that effect! It was great that he phoned me right away to congratulate me and to find out how it went, this meant a huge amount to me. What a day! This run was personally especially important to me. Having had several significant DNF's since my return to running, it was imperative for my motivation and my mental health that I succeeded. This run allows me to say, 'I might not look like an ultrarunner, but I am'!

Although I ran twice the distance at the Watchtree 100mph event the previous year, this run holds a higher significance in my mind. The Watchtree event was still a good achievement, but because It consisted of a few laps of the very flat nature reserve followed by a ten to twenty minute break (and repeat) and it didn't have challenges of technical terrain, elevation or continuous effort that my run from Keswick to Carlisle threw at me, it didn't require the amount of continuous effort and mental strength that attracts me to ultra running. I was very happy with my achievement at Watchtree, but I would not have felt comfortable if I said it marked my much-needed return to ultra running. My run from Keswick to Carlisle qualified me to call myself an ultrarunner again in my mind at least, and it definitely felt good to be back! I began trying to understand how and why this ultra distance had gone so amazingly well. I certainly did not have any definitive answers, but I definitely had a few plausible theories.

The coaching and guidance from Paul and my consistency throughout the training block meant that I was starting the run in the best trail running shape I had been in for an exceptionally long time. Something else that Paul had worked on me with was nutrition. So, for this challenge I had a solid nutrition schedule in place, and I stuck to it stringently. I also had a backup plan just in case things went awry, so when my stomach started to refuse the gels, I had some back up fuel that I knew I could cope with. Because of this I had great energy levels for the full route, which meant I could continue with an efficient leg turnover for the duration of the distance.

My mind, surprisingly, was a contributing factor into my positive experience throughout the adventure. The day before I ran, I was quite stressed about what was ahead of me. I questioned my ability,

I doubted whether I was capable of the distance, and I was convinced that my navigational skills would let me down. All this self-defeating negativity was standard fare for me, which was why my continual and unwavering positivity and high energy through the duration of my run was very puzzling. This was the first long distance run that I had done where I was super happy at every part, there was no self-doubt, no doubting my ability and no dark thoughts. This was not what I was used to, but I certainly liked it!

As I intimated earlier, I did have an idea what the cause of all the positive mental balance was. At this stage in my life, I was learning to become more aware of some of my bipolar symptoms. This enabled me to believe that I was on the cusp of a hypomanic episode. This was a little worrying of course, but during that moment it was having a positive impact on me. I did not know if it was possible to harness the power of an episode, but I was determined to just relax into this one and see what happened. My theory was certainly correct as a few days later the physical and mental symptoms of a hypomanic episode became unignorably obvious!

Trail, fell, and ultra-running gives me so much, particularly when I remove any unnecessary pressure. It allows me to work towards exciting goals that should be bigger than me. This type of running takes me to beautiful places and enables to feel close to nature. More importantly it helps me manage my condition, by keeping me grounded and in the moment.

Since my successful ultra distance run, I have had some much-needed recovery time, and I began training for my next big ultra distance challenge. I never thought I would say this, but it just might be fun times ahead!

The reality of my condition was that bipolar would always be an incredibly significant part of my life as it already had been for more years than I cared to remember. I spent a huge amount of my energy trying to find that silver bullet that would enable me to live a normal life. I was always compliant with my psychiatric medication and my mental health appointments, I always worked hard on my cognitive behavioural therapy sessions, and I spent a large number of time, seeking out peer reviewed research and participated in ongoing studies. One such study I was involved with was run by the School of Psychology at the University of East London. The purpose study was to ascertain whether transcranial direct current stimulation therapy would be effective in treating bipolar depressive symptoms from home. My participation in this study required me to place a device onto my head which sent a low electrical current to my brain for thirty minutes five times a week. Yes, I was that desperate that I volunteered have my brain regularly electrocuted! In all seriousness though, it was not as bad as it sounds. Some patients will not even feel the current. For me it was like an electrical tickle and a mild itch. Surprising a sensation most like being tattooed than anything else. I think that the therapy did improve my mood, but only marginally. I continued my search for my cure, but it unsurprisingly always eluded me. I did eventually turn a corner with how I looked at my personal flavour of bipolar, and this came from an unlikely but major area of my life, running!

I mentioned in a previous chapter that because of my long-term physical health problems, I had to rethink how I looked at my running. I had to stop getting frustrated with my pace (or lack of) and how difficult I found hills. I knew that I had to accept my limitations and focus on what I was capable of, such as endurance running and spending more time running on trails and mountains.

Having rediscovered my pure enjoyment for running some incredible adventure lay ahead. This new direction triggered a massive change in how I perceived my bipolar diagnosis, and more specifically how I saw my life with bipolar. The key aspect of this was acceptance. I had to accept that bipolar was part of who I am and always would be, for better or for worse. I had to accept that I

223

would always experience depressive episodes as well as manic or hypomanic ones. Finally, I had to accept that in basic terms, where my symptoms were at that point in time, was as good as it was going to get. This was not a case of giving up the fight, but more of accepting that things were not going to improve significantly through medication treatment or therapy. It was not a negative realisation for me, it was quite freeing. I knew that I had to take control of my condition and ultimately, my life.

It was around thirty years since my first bipolar symptoms manifested and ten years or so since my diagnosis, I really wished that what I know now, I knew back at the beginning. My life could have run a lot smoother!

I hope that it will be useful to someone recently diagnosed with bipolar (or someone caring for someone with bipolar), to read some of my thoughts about what I wish I knew about the condition and treatment at the time of my diagnosis. This is based on my firsthand experiences of both my care and my version of bipolar, so whilst I hope some of it resonates with some of you, it may not mirror your exact experiences.

Medication: The thing with bipolar medication is that different people can react to medications in different ways (or not at all). One person may get problematic side effects from a drug that someone else might be perfectly fine with. Just as one person may experience positive therapeutic effects whilst someone else might not. For example, a couple of medications I am currently taking, cause me to frequently have blurry vision, yet I know many people who take the same prescribed drugs, and they have no side effects at all. It is not a one size fits all scenario; the key here is to be prepared to be patient. It can take a lot of trial and error to get the right mix of medications that work well for you. Remember that none of the currently available bipolar medications will cure you of your symptoms, I am sorry, but this is the truth. The medication that you will likely need to take is quite simply just one tool in your arsenal that should help you manage your condition. Some people do successfully manage their condition without medication, but they are in the minority unfortunately.

Mental Health Services: Within the UK at least, the standard of care you receive can be a bit of a lottery. This is more due to a severe lack of funding than anything else. I felt quite privileged to have access to the community mental health team in Cumbria, even though there were a few bumps along the way. My main piece of advice here would be to try and not be too reliant on the service. If you do, you may feel frequently let down. Self-reliance is what will benefit you in the long run.

Physical Health: As I mentioned in a previous chapter people with bipolar are more likely to get conditions like heart disease, type 2 diabetes, and obesity. Many of these risks seem to stem from lifestyle or medication side effects. To give yourself a chance of avoiding some of these conditions it may well pay to research and understand the available psychiatric medications. Try to opt for weight neutral options if they are available. Trying to put healthy eating and regular physical activity into your routine will help you both physically and mentally.

You are not alone: For me, having bipolar has at times been an isolating experience. I felt I could not relate to anyone around me. Nobody thought the way I did and even others with same condition seemed to have different symptoms to me. The reality is that as humans, every single one of us is unique, with people with psychiatric conditions like bipolar, our uniqueness is just more noticeable than most others. It is our uniqueness that gives us that important common ground together.

The fact that I have bipolar is not my fault, so this has enabled me to feel comfortable talking openly about it. This has helped me cope with having the condition in the last few decades. When you start to be open about your life with bipolar, there will be some people that don't quite know how to react to your revelation, but most will be understanding. My advice here would be to try and find someone you feel comfortable talking to about some of the more personal aspects of your life. This has certainly helped me over the years.

Where I find myself now with both my bipolar diagnosis and my life in general, is possibly in the most positive and optimistic space I have ever been in. The two main reasons for this are my more accepting view of my diagnosis and the fact that I have become a lot more self-aware of my symptoms.

Being self-aware means that I can identify most progressing manic or hypomanic episodes before they go supernova! This enables me to forewarn Kath, so she can keep an eye on me and hopefully stop me from getting out of control. I am under no illusion here, I know I will always have depressive and manic episodes, and I will struggle with my life intensely at times. However, by keeping things simpler and sticking to a regular daily routine I should avoid many triggers for potential bipolar episodes and increase my enjoyment of life outside of my symptoms. I find myself more positive and excited about my future than I have been for what seems like an age. So much so, despite my obvious anxiety of returning to work, I have just applied for my first job in around fifteen years. I don't know if I am ready for this huge step, but I'm not sure if I will ever feel ready. You have to take the plunge sometime, don't you?

Alpine Catchfly in the Coledale Fells

The lone Scots Pine on the Cumbria Way

High Pike Summit

Celebration at Carlisle Castle

The best support crew.

Appendix A
Mental Health Resources

Please note that I cannot personally recommend all these mental health resources as I have only engaged with some in the UK, this rather limited list should be regarded as a guide to what may be available for you, should you need support. This is not an exhaustive list. If your country is not featured here, you should find local services through a quick internet search.

Mental Health Services (UK)

Accident and Emergency (Phone 999)
Samaritans (Phone 116 123) or email jo@samaritans.org
SANELine (Phone 0300 304 7000 4.30pm to 10.30pm daily)
National Suicide Prevention Helpline UK (Phone 0800 689 5652 6pm to midnight every day)
SHOUT (Text 85258)

Mental Health Services (Ireland)

Mental Health Ireland (Phone 01 2841166)
Aware Depression & Bipolar Disorder Support (Phone 1800 80 48 48)

Grow mental health support (Phone 1890 474 474)
Shine supporting people affected by mental ill health
(Phone 01 541 3715)

Useful web-based resources

International Bipolar Foundation - https://ibpf.org/
BP Hope - https://www.bphope.com/
Bipolar UK https://www.bipolaruk.org/
Depression and Bipolar Support Alliance -
https://www.dbsalliance.org/
Mind - https://www.mind.org.uk/
Campaign Against Living Miserably:
https://www.thecalmzone.net/

Appendix B
Birding Resources

This is a list of birding resources that I have either mentioned in this book or believe they would be of use to anyone that wishes to learn more about birds, birding, or bird conservation.

National and international birding and wildlife organisations

British Trust for Ornithology (BTO)
https://www.bto.org/
Royal Society for the Protection of Birds (RSPB)
https://www.rspb.org.uk/
Birdlife International https://www.birdlife.org/
British Ornithologists Union (BOU) https://bou.org.uk/
British Birds Rarities Committee (BBRC)
https://www.bbrc.org.uk/
Irish Rare Birds Committee (IRBC) http://www.irbc.ie/
Scottish Ornithologists Club (SOC)
https://www.thesoc.org.uk/
Society for the Protection of Nature in Israel (SPNI)

https://natureisrael.org/
Batumi Raptor Count (BRC)
https://www.batumiraptorcount.org/
Society for Nature Conservation (SABUKO) (Republic of Georgia) https://www.sabuko.org/en/
Biotope (Arctic Norway) https://www.biotope.no/
Doğa Derneği (Nature Society of Türkiye)
https://www.dogadernegi.org/

Other useful birding resources

Birdforum https://www.birdforum.net/
British Birds https://britishbirds.co.uk/
BUBO Listing https://bubo.org/
Birdguides https://www.birdguides.com/
Rare Bird Alert https://www.rarebirdalert.co.uk/
Surbirds http://surfbirds.com/index.php

Some amazing birding sites, both home and away

Spurn Bird Observatory
https://spurnbirdobservatory.co.uk/
Fair Isle Bird Observatory
http://www.fairislebirdobs.co.uk/
Isles of Scilly Bird Group (ISBG)
https://www.scillybirding.co.uk/
Cape Clear Bird Observatory
https://birdwatchireland.ie/our-work/cape-clear-birdobservatory/
Varanger Birding http://www.varanger.net
Daylan Birding (Türkiye) https://dalyanbirding.com/

Hula Valley Nature Reserve (Israel)
https://en.parks.org.il/reserve-park/hula-nature-reserve/#13
Batumi Birding (Georgia) https://batumibirding.com/
Birding in Spain https://www.birdinginspain.com/

Appendix C
My Bird List

This is a complete list of every full species of bird that I was lucky enough to see in the UK and Ireland during the period I spent as an active birder and twitcher. This list is in taxonomical order rather than chronological order.

- Snow Goose (Anser caerulescens)
- Ross's Goose (Anser rossii)
- Graylag Goose (Anser anser)
- Greater White-fronted Goose (Anser albifrons)
- Lesser White-fronted Goose (Anser erythropus)
- Taiga Bean-Goose (Anser fabalis)
- Tundra Bean-Goose (Anser serrirostris)
- Pink-footed Goose (Anser brachyrhynchus)
- Brent Goose (Branta bernicla)
- Barnacle Goose (Branta leucopsis)
- Cackling Goose (Branta hutchinsii)
- Canada Goose (Branta canadensis)
- Red-breasted Goose (Branta ruficollis)
- Mute Swan (Cygnus olor)
- Bewick's Swan (Cygnus columbianus)
- Whooper Swan (Cygnus cygnus)
- Egyptian Goose (Alopochen aegyptiaca)
- Ruddy Shelduck (Tadorna ferruginea)
- Common Shelduck (Tadorna tadorna)
- Mandarin Duck (Aix galericulata)
- Garganey (Spatula querquedula)

- Blue-winged Teal (Spatula discors)
- Northern Shoveler (Spatula clypeata)
- Gadwall (Mareca strepera)
- Eurasian Wigeon (Mareca penelope)
- American Wigeon (Mareca americana)
- Mallard (Anas platyrhynchos)
- American Black Duck (Anas rubripes)
- Northern Pintail (Anas acuta)
- Green-winged Teal (Anas crecca)
- Red-crested Pochard (Netta rufina)
- Common Pochard (Aythya ferina)
- Ring-necked Duck (Aythya collaris)
- Ferruginous Duck (Aythya nyroca)
- Tufted Duck (Aythya fuligula)
- Greater Scaup (Aythya marila)
- Lesser Scaup (Aythya affinis)
- King Eider (Somateria spectabilis)
- Common Eider (Somateria mollissima)
- Harlequin Duck (Histrionicus histrionicus)
- Surf Scoter (Melanitta perspicillata)
- Velvet Scoter (Melanitta fusca)
- Stejneger's Scoter (Melanitta stejnegeri)
- Common Scoter (Melanitta nigra)
- Black Scoter (Melanitta americana)
- Long-tailed Duck (Clangula hyemalis)
- Bufflehead (Bucephala albeola)
- Common Goldeneye (Bucephala clangula)
- Barrow's Goldeneye (Bucephala islandica)
- Smew (Mergellus albellus)
- Hooded Merganser (Lophodytes cucullatus)
- Common Merganser (Mergus merganser)
- Red-breasted Merganser (Mergus serrator)
- Ruddy Duck (Oxyura jamaicensis)
- White-headed Duck (Oxyura leucocephala)
- Willow Ptarmigan (Lagopus lagopus)
- Rock Ptarmigan (Lagopus muta)
- Western Capercaillie (Tetrao urogallus)
- Black Grouse (Lyrurus tetrix)
- Grey Partridge (Perdix perdix)
- Golden Pheasant (Chrysolophus pictus)
- Ring-necked Pheasant (Phasianus colchicus)
- Common Quail (Coturnix coturnix)

- Red-legged Partridge (Alectoris rufa)
- Little Grebe (Tachybaptus ruficollis)
- Pied-billed Grebe (Podilymbus podiceps)
- Slavonian Grebe (Podiceps auritus)
- Red-necked Grebe (Podiceps grisegena)
- Great Crested Grebe (Podiceps cristatus)
- Black-necked Grebe (Podiceps nigricollis)
- Rock Pigeon (Columba livia)
- Stock Dove (Columba oenas)
- Common Wood-Pigeon (Columba palumbus)
- European Turtle-Dove (Streptopelia turtur)
- Oriental Turtle-Dove (Streptopelia orientalis)
- Eurasian Collared-Dove (Streptopelia decaocto)
- Great Spotted Cuckoo (Clamator glandarius)
- Common Cuckoo (Cuculus canorus)
- Eurasian Nightjar (Caprimulgus europaeus)
- Chimney Swift (Chaetura pelagica)
- Alpine Swift (Apus melba)
- Common Swift (Apus apus)
- Pallid Swift (Apus pallidus)
- Water Rail (Rallus aquaticus)
- Corn Crake (Crex crex)
- Sora (Porzana carolina)
- Spotted Crake (Porzana porzana)
- Eurasian Moorhen (Gallinula chloropus)
- Eurasian Coot (Fulica atra)
- American Coot (Fulica americana)
- Baillon's Crake (Zapornia pusilla)
- Sandhill Crane (Antigone canadensis)
- Common Crane (Grus grus)
- Stone Curlew (Burhinus oedicnemus)
- Black-winged Stilt (Himantopus himantopus)
- Pied Avocet (Recurvirostra avosetta)
- Eurasian Oystercatcher (Haematopus ostralegus)
- Grey Plover (Pluvialis squatarola)
- European Golden-Plover (Pluvialis apricaria)
- American Golden-Plover (Pluvialis dominica)
- Pacific Golden-Plover (Pluvialis fulva)
- Northern Lapwing (Vanellus vanellus)

- Sociable Lapwing (Vanellus gregarius)
- White-tailed Lapwing (Vanellus leucurus)
- Lesser Sand-Plover (Charadrius mongolus)
- Greater Sand-Plover (Charadrius leschenaultii)
- Common Ringed Plover (Charadrius hiaticula)
- Little Ringed Plover (Charadrius dubius)
- Eurasian Dotterel (Charadrius morinellus)
- Upland Sandpiper (Bartramia longicauda)
- Whimbrel (Numenius phaeopus)
- Eurasian Curlew (Numenius arquata)
- Bar-tailed Godwit (Limosa lapponica)
- Black-tailed Godwit (Limosa limosa)
- Ruddy Turnstone (Arenaria interpres)
- Great Knot (Calidris tenuirostris)
- Knot (Calidris canutus)
- Ruff (Calidris pugnax)
- Broad-billed Sandpiper (Calidris falcinellus)
- Stilt Sandpiper (Calidris himantopus)
- Curlew Sandpiper (Calidris ferruginea)
- Temminck's Stint (Calidris temminckii)
- Sanderling (Calidris alba)
- Dunlin (Calidris alpina)
- Purple Sandpiper (Calidris maritima)
- Baird's Sandpiper (Calidris bairdii)
- Little Stint (Calidris minuta)
- Least Sandpiper (Calidris minutilla)
- White-rumped Sandpiper (Calidris fuscicollis)
- Buff-breasted Sandpiper (Calidris subruficollis)
- Pectoral Sandpiper (Calidris melanotos)
- Semipalmated Sandpiper (Calidris pusilla)
- Western Sandpiper (Calidris mauri)
- Short-billed Dowitcher (Limnodromus griseus)
- Long-billed (DowitcherLimnodromus scolopaceus)
- Jack Snipe (Lymnocryptes minimus)
- Eurasian Woodcock (Scolopax rusticola)
- Great Snipe (Gallinago media)
- Common Snipe (Gallinago gallinago)
- Terek Sandpiper (Xenus cinereus)
- Wilson's Phalarope (Phalaropus tricolor)
- Red-necked Phalarope (Phalaropus lobatus)

- Grey Phalarope (Phalaropus fulicarius)
- Common Sandpiper (Actitis hypoleucos)
- Spotted Sandpiper (Actitis macularius)
- Green Sandpiper (Tringa ochropus)
- Solitary Sandpiper (Tringa solitaria)
- Spotted Redshank (Tringa erythropus)
- Greater Yellowlegs (Tringa melanoleuca)
- Common Greenshank (Tringa nebularia)
- Lesser Yellowlegs (Tringa flavipes)
- Marsh Sandpiper (Tringa stagnatilis)
- Wood Sandpiper (Tringa glareola)
- Common Redshank (Tringa totanus)
- Cream-coloured Courser (Cursorius cursor)
- Oriental Pratincole (Glareola maldivarum)
- Black-winged Pratincole (Glareola nordmanni)
- Great Skua (Stercorarius skua)
- Pomarine Skua (Stercorarius pomarinus)
- Arctic Skua (Stercorarius parasiticus)
- Long-tailed Skua (Stercorarius longicaudus)
- Little Auk (Alle alle)
- Common Guillemot (Uria aalge)
- Razorbill (Alca torda)
- Atlantic Puffin (Fratercula arctica)
- Black-legged Kittiwake (Rissa tridactyla)
- Ivory Gull (Pagophila eburnea)
- Sabine's Gull (Xema sabini)
- Bonaparte's Gull (Chroicocephalus philadelphia)
- Black-headed Gull (Chroicocephalus ridibundus)
- Little Gull (Hydrocoloeus minutus)
- Ross's Gull (Rhodostethia rosea)
- Laughing Gull (Leucophaeus atricilla)
- Franklin's Gull (Leucophaeus pipixcan)
- Mediterranean Gull (Ichthyaetus melanocephalus)
- Common Gull (Larus canus)
- Ring-billed Gull (Larus delawarensis)
- Herring Gull (Larus argentatus)
- American Herring Gull (Larus smithsinianus)
- Yellow-legged Gull (Larus michahellis)
- Caspian Gull (Larus cachinnans)

- Iceland Gull (Larus glaucoides)
- Lesser Black-backed Gull (Larus fuscus)
- Slaty-backed Gull (Larus schistisagus)
- Glaucous-winged Gull (Larus glaucescens)
- Glaucous Gull (Larus hyperboreus)
- Great Black-backed Gull (Larus marinus)
- Sooty Tern (Onychoprion fuscatus)
- Little Tern (Sternula albifrons)
- Caspian Tern (Hydroprogne caspia)
- Black Tern (Chlidonias niger)
- White-winged Tern (Chlidonias leucopterus)
- Whiskered Tern (Chlidonias hybrida)
- Roseate Tern (Sterna dougallii)
- Common Tern (Sterna hirundo)
- Arctic Tern (Sterna paradisaea)
- Forster's Tern (Sterna forsteri)
- Sandwich Tern (Thalasseus sandvicensis)
- Elegant Tern (Thalasseus elegans)
- Red-throated Diver (Gavia stellata)
- Arctic Diver (Gavia arctica)
- Pacific Diver (Gavia pacifica)
- Common Diver (Gavia immer)
- Yellow-billed Diver (Gavia adamsii)
- Wilson's Storm-Petrel (Oceanites oceanicus)
- European Storm-Petrel (Hydrobates pelagicus)
- Leach's Storm-Petrel (Hydrobates leucorhous)
- Northern Fulmar (Fulmarus glacialis)
- Cory's Shearwater (Calonectris diomedea)
- Great Shearwater (Ardenna gravis)
- Sooty Shearwater (Ardenna grisea)
- Manx Shearwater (Puffinus puffinus)
- Balearic Shearwater (Puffinus mauretanicus)
- Black Stork (Ciconia nigra)
- White Stork (Ciconia ciconia)
- Northern Gannet (Morus bassanus)
- Great Cormorant (Phalacrocorax carbo)
- European Shag (Gulosus aristotelis)
- Great Bittern (Botaurus stellaris)
- Grey Heron (Ardea cinerea)
- Purple Heron (Ardea purpurea)
- Great Egret (Ardea alba)

- Little Egret (Egretta garzetta)
- Snowy Egret (Egretta thula)
- Cattle Egret (Bubulcus ibis)
- Squacco Heron (Ardeola ralloides)
- Green Heron (Butorides virescens)
- Black-crowned Night-Heron (Nycticorax nycticorax)
- Glossy Ibis (Plegadis falcinellus)
- Eurasian Spoonbill (Platalea leucorodia)
- Osprey (Pandion haliaetus)
- Booted Eagle (Hieraaetus pennatus)
- Golden Eagle (Aquila chrysaetos)
- Eurasian Marsh-Harrier (Circus aeruginosus)
- Hen Harrier (Circus cyaneus)
- Northern Harrier (Circus hudsonius)
- Pallid Harrier (Circus macrourus)
- Montagu's Harrier (Circus pygargus)
- Eurasian Sparrowhawk (Accipiter nisus)
- Northern Goshawk (Accipiter gentilis)
- Red Kite (Milvus milvus)
- Black Kite (Milvus migrans)
- White-tailed Eagle (Haliaeetus albicilla)
- Rough-legged Buzzard (Buteo lagopus)
- Common Buzzard (Buteo buteo)
- Eurasian Kestrel (Falco tinnunculus)
- Red-footed Falcon (Falco vespertinus)
- Merlin (Falco columbarius)
- Eurasian Hobby (Falco subbuteo)
- Gyrfalcon (Falco rusticolus)
- Peregrine Falcon (Falco peregrinus)
- Barn Owl (Tyto alba)
- Eurasian Scops-Owl (Otus scops)
- Little Owl (Athene noctua)
- Tawny Owl (Strix aluco)
- Long-eared Owl (Asio otus)
- Short-eared Owl (Asio flammeus)
- Eurasian Hoopoe (Upupa epops)
- Common Kingfisher (Alcedo atthis)
- Belted Kingfisher (Megaceryle alcyon)
- European Bee-eater (Merops apiaster)
- European Roller (Coracias garrulus)
- Eurasian Wryneck (Jynx torquilla)
- Great Spotted Woodpecker (Dendrocopos major)

- Lesser Spotted Woodpecker (Dryobates minor)
- Eurasian Green Woodpecker (Picus viridis)
- Rose-ringed Parakeet (Psittacula krameri)
- Alder Flycatcher (Empidonax alnorum)
- Red-eyed Vireo (Vireo olivaceus)
- Eurasian Golden Oriole (Oriolus oriolus)
- Red-backed Shrike (Lanius collurio)
- Red-tailed Shrike (Lanius phoenicuroides)
- Isabelline Shrike (Lanius isabellinus)
- Great Grey Shrike (Lanius excubitor)
- Lesser Grey Shrike (Lanius minor)
- Masked Shrike (Lanius nubicus)
- Woodchat Shrike (Lanius senator)
- Eurasian Jay (Garrulus glandarius)
- Eurasian Magpie (Pica pica)
- Red-billed Chough (Pyrrhocorax pyrrhocorax)
- Eurasian Jackdaw (Corvus monedula)
- Rook (Corvus frugilegus)
- Carrion Crow (Corvus corone)
- Hooded Crow (Corvus cornix)
- Common Raven (Corvus corax)
- Coal Tit (Periparus ater)
- Crested Tit (Lophophanes cristatus)
- Marsh Tit (Poecile palustris)
- Willow Tit (Poecile montanus)
- Blue Tit (Cyanistes caeruleus)
- Great Tit (Parus major)
- Long-tailed Tit (Aegithalos caudatus)
- Shore Lark (Eremophila alpestris)
- Greater Short-toed Lark (Calandrella brachydactyla)
- Black Lark (Melanocorypha yeltoniensis)
- Wood Lark (Lullula arborea)
- Eurasian Skylark (Alauda arvensis)
- Bearded Reedling (Panurus biarmicus)
- Booted Warbler (Iduna caligata)
- Sykes's Warbler (Iduna rama)
- Eastern Olivaceous Warbler (Iduna pallida)
- Melodious Warbler (Hippolais polyglotta)
- Icterine Warbler (Hippolais icterina)

- Aquatic Warbler (Acrocephalus paludicola)
- Sedge Warbler (Acrocephalus schoenobaenus)
- Paddyfield Warbler (Acrocephalus agricola)
- Blyth's Reed Warbler (Acrocephalus dumetorum)
- Marsh Warbler (Acrocephalus palustris)
- Common Reed Warbler (Acrocephalus
- scirpaceus)
- Great Reed Warbler (Acrocephalus arundinaceus)
- Savi's Warbler (Locustella luscinioides)
- Common Grasshopper Warbler (Locustella naevia)
- Sand Martin (Riparia riparia)
- Barn Swallow (Hirundo rustica)
- Red-rumped Swallow (Cecropis daurica)
- Common House-Martin (Delichon urbicum)
- Wood Warbler (Phylloscopus sibilatrix)
- Western Bonelli's Warbler (Phylloscopus bonelli)
- Yellow-browed Warbler (Phylloscopus inornatus)
- Hume's Warbler (Phylloscopus humei)
- Pallas's Warbler (Phylloscopus proregulus)
- Radde's Warbler (Phylloscopus schwarzi)
- Dusky Warbler (Phylloscopus fuscatus)
- Willow Warbler (Phylloscopus trochilus)
- Common Chiffchaff (Phylloscopus collybita)
- Iberian Chiffchaff (Phylloscopus ibericus)
- Eastern Crowned Warbler (Phylloscopus coronatus)
- Greenish Warbler (Phylloscopus trochiloides)
- Two-barred Warbler (Phylloscopus plumbeitarsus)
- Arctic Warbler (Phylloscopus borealis)
- Cetti's Warbler (Cettia cetti)
- Eurasian Blackcap (Sylvia atricapilla)
- Garden Warbler (Sylvia borin)
- Barred Warbler (Curruca nisoria)
- Lesser Whitethroat (Curruca curruca)

- Western Orphean Warbler (Curruca hortensis)
- Asian Desert Warbler (Curruca nana)
- Sardinian Warbler (Curruca melanocephala)
- Western Subalpine Warbler (Curruca iberiae)
- Eastern Subalpine Warbler (Curruca cantillans)
- Common Whitethroat (Curruca communis)
- Marmora's Warbler (Curruca sarda)
- Dartford Warbler (Curruca undata)
- Goldcrest (Regulus regulus)
- Common Firecrest (Regulus ignicapilla)
- Eurasian Nuthatch (Sitta europaea)
- Eurasian Treecreeper (Certhia familiaris)
- Short-toed Treecreeper (Certhia brachydactyla)
- Eurasian Wren (Troglodytes troglodytes)
- Dipper (Cinclus cinclus)
- European Starling (Sturnus vulgaris)
- Rosy Starling (Pastor roseus)
- White's Thrush (Zoothera aurea)
- Gray-cheeked Thrush (Catharus minimus)
- Mistle Thrush (Turdus viscivorus)
- Song Thrush (Turdus philomelos)
- Redwing (Turdus iliacus)
- Eurasian Blackbird (Turdus merula)
- American Robin (Turdus migratorius)
- Fieldfare (Turdus pilaris)
- Ring Ouzel (Turdus torquatus)
- Black-throated Thrush (Turdus atrogularis)
- Spotted Flycatcher (Muscicapa striata)
- European Robin (Erithacus rubecula)
- White-throated Robin (Irania gutturalis)
- Thrush Nightingale (Luscinia luscinia)
- Common Nightingale (Luscinia megarhynchos)
- Bluethroat (Luscinia svecica)
- Red-flanked Bluetail (Tarsiger cyanurus)
- Taiga Flycatcher (Ficedula albicilla)
- Red-breasted Flycatcher (Ficedula parva)
- European Pied Flycatcher (Ficedula hypoleuca)
- Collared Flycatcher (Ficedula albicollis)
- Common Redstart (Phoenicurus phoenicurus)

- Black Redstart (Phoenicurus ochruros)
- Whinchat (Saxicola rubetra)
- European Stonechat (Saxicola rubicola)
- Siberian Stonechat (Saxicola maurus)
- Northern Wheatear (Oenanthe oenanthe)
- Desert Wheatear (Oenanthe deserti)
- Western (Black-eared Wheatear)
- Pied Wheatear (Oenanthe pleschanka)
- Bohemian Waxwing (Bombycilla garrulus)
- Dunnock (Prunella modularis)
- House Sparrow (Passer domesticus)
- Spanish Sparrow (Passer hispaniolensis)
- Eurasian Tree Sparrow (Passer montanus)
- Grey Wagtail (Motacilla cinerea)
- Western Yellow Wagtail (Motacilla flava)
- Citrine Wagtail (Motacilla citreola)
- Pied Wagtail (Motacilla alba)
- Richard's Pipit (Anthus richardi)
- Tawny Pipit (Anthus campestris)
- Meadow Pipit (Anthus pratensis)
- Tree Pipit (Anthus trivialis)

- Olive-backed Pipit (Anthus hodgsoni)
- Red-throated Pipit (Anthus cervinus)
- Water Pipit (Anthus spinoletta)
- Rock Pipit (Anthus petrosus)
- American Buff-bellied Pipit (Anthus rubescens)
- Common Chaffinch (Fringilla coelebs)
- Brambling (Fringilla montifringilla)
- Hawfinch (Coccothraustes coccothraustes)
- Common Rosefinch (Carpodacus erythrinus)
- Eurasian Bullfinch (Pyrrhula pyrrhula)
- European Greenfinch (Chloris chloris)
- Twite (Linaria flavirostris)
- Eurasian Linnet (Linaria cannabina)
- Common Redpoll (Acanthis flammea)
- Lesser Redpoll (Acanthis cabaret)
- Coues's Arctic Redpoll (Acanthis exilipes)
- Parrot Crossbill (Loxia pytyopsittacus)
- Crossbill (Loxia curvirostra)
- Two-barred Crossbill (Loxia leucoptera)
- European Goldfinch (Carduelis carduelis)

- European Serin
  (Serinus serinus)
- Eurasian Siskin
  (Spinus spinus)
- Lapland Longspur
  (Calcarius lapponicus)
- Snow Bunting
  (Plectrophenax nivalis)
- Black-headed Bunting
  (Emberiza
  melanocephala)
- Corn Bunting
  (Emberiza calandra)
- Cirl Bunting (Emberiza
  cirlus)
- Yellowhammer
  (Emberiza citrinella)
- Pine Bunting
  (Emberiza
  leucocephalos)
- Ortolan Bunting
  (Emberiza hortulana)
- Reed Bunting
  (Emberiza schoeniclus)
- Yellow-breasted
  Bunting (Emberiza
  aureola)
- Little Bunting
  (Emberiza pusilla)
- Rustic Bunting
  (Emberiza rustica)
- Black-faced Bunting
  (Emberiza
  spodocephala)
- White-crowned
  Sparrow (Zonotrichia
  leucophry)
- White-throated
  Sparrow (Zonotrichia
  albicollis)
- Baltimore Oriole
  (Icterus galbula)
- Blue-winged Warbler
  (Vermivora
  cyanoptera)
- Blackpoll Warbler
  (Setophaga striata)
- Myrtle Warbler
  (Setophaga coronata)

Appendix D
Running Resources

Summit Ultra Coaching
https://summitultra.co.uk/coaching
Bob Graham 24-hour Club
http://bobgrahamclub.org.uk/
Steve Parr Round
https://gofar997.wixsite.com/gofar/steveparr-round
George Fisher Tea Round
https://www.georgefisher.co.uk/tearound
Fell Runners Association https://www.fellrunner.org.uk/
Trail Runners Association https://www.tra-uk.org/
Sientries Events List https://www.sientries.co.uk/
Go Far Ultra Distance Challenges
http://www.gofar.org.uk/
Northern Fells Running Club (NFRC)
https://www.northernfellsrc.org.uk/

Big Thanks

Firstly, I want to thank Kath, for so many things; but mostly because she has stuck with me despite my obvious short comings. My three wonderful daughters, Shannon, Erin, and Thea are next in the acknowledgments for making my life so much richer, and for their undeniable excitement for life. My son Lachlan must get a mention for always making my life interesting. Sam Starmer gets massive recognition for his amazing friendship, always being there for me whatever type brand of bipolar symptoms I am stuck in and for joining me for so many adventures. Chris Hind and Peter Birkett I thank for their friendship and company on many birding trips, despite my mental health struggles. Derek Charles for an incredible friendship, taking me to see some fantastic birds across the Irish Sea and for introducing me to overseas birding. Martin Garner and Sharon get a huge thanks for their beautiful friendship, for seeing something special in me, encouraging my passion for bird identification and enabling me to travel to Arctic Norway and Israel. I miss Martin so much.

I cannot move on without giving both Ian Simms and Mike Doughty-Lee a big thanks for all the twitching adventures that we shared. During my birding trips overseas, I met some very special people such as Yoav Perlman, Jonathan Meyrav, Vincent van der Spek and Tormod Amundsen who I had some great wildlife experiences with.

My friend Charlie Moores gets a special mention for inspiring my wildlife conservation passion and for being the friend that I needed at that point of my life. Ceri Levi and Ralph Steadman deserve a big thanks from me, for allowing me to be part of their very creative conservation initiative. John Miles gets a special mention for dropping by for a chat during some very tough times for me.

When it comes to my tattoo phase, my biggest thanks goes to Richard Batey for his amazing artistic skills and his infectious enthusiasm for life.

There are a huge number of people who have cheered me on and supported me during my running 'career' thus far and I am very grateful to all of them. Out of these people I must give acknowledgement to Lindsey and Andrew Graham and, Steve Claringbold who gave me so much encouragement from my first Parkrun and have continued to do ever since. Along the same vein, Paul 'Dobbo' Dobson, Andrew Martindale, Robert Johnstone, Richard 'Nobby' Noble, Natalie Hawkrigg, Rose Singleton, Chris Curtis, Anna Blackburn, Lindsay Walker, Claire Dickinson, Dave Dicks, Jo May, Angela Wilson, Ian Grimshaw, Stephen Wilson, Gaynor Prior, Richard Todd, Dave, and Morag Thomson and, Howard Seal for their continuous support and encouragement. I cannot close out the running section without giving big props to my coach, Paul Wilson. Paul is a brilliant and knowledgeable coach and has given me so much encouragement and that has enabled me to achieve far more than I ever anticipated.

Last but by no means least I must thank Healthy Hopes who have given me a huge amount of help and support when I really needed it; and the Community Mental Health Team who have given me some vital help and support during my time working with them.

Thank you to everyone who has been there for me in both tough and happy times.

The Author

Tristan Reid is a former twitcher, bird photographer and wildlife conservation activist. Having found employment in a varied range of wildlife related industries, and supplemented this with a lifelong interest in nature, he has built up a good knowledge of the subject. '**You Don't Look Like an Ultra Runner**' is Tristan's first venture into self-publishing, but he has contributed to other books, including, '**Where to watch birds in Northwest England**' (AC & Black 2008) and the groundbreaking collaboration '**Red Sixty-Seven**' (British Trust for Ornithology 2020)

Tristan is a mental health advocate who has been very open about his own diagnosis of bipolar. This condition has thrown up both exciting and adventures and very difficult episodes for Tristan, but he has drawn some comfort and respite as a very unlikely ultrarunner. Prior to the publication of his book, Tristan is probably best known for getting both his arms tattooed to raise funds for **Turkish wildlife**, and for running fourteen marathons during 2014 to raise funds for **Operation Turtle Dove**. Alongside these creative conservation fundraising projects, Tristan became an experienced public speaker, giving talks and lectures across the UK and overseas.

Please consider leaving a review of this book on Amazon, either via the link below or via the **QR** code provided. Thank you.

Link to reviews page: https://tinyurl.com/ReviewUltraRun

QR Code

Printed in Great Britain
by Amazon

44312504R00145